ISRAEL'S HOLY MOEDIM

ISRAEL'S HOLY MOEDIM

and their prophetic significance today

Peter Sammons

Glory to Glory Publications

First published in Great Britain by
Glory to Glory Publications
an imprint of
Buy Research Ltd., Salisbury House, Station Road, Cambridge, CB1 2LA

ISBN 978-0-9926674-6-7

Printed in Great Britain by Imprint Digital, Exeter
and worldwide by CreateSpace

Contents

Dedicated to the memory of

Violet Ruth Sammons

1921–2016

I trust in your unfailing love;
my heart rejoices in your salvation.
I will sing to the Lord,
for he has been good to me.

(Psalm 13:5–6)

PREFACE

In order to plan a successful journey most would want to study a map. Peter Sammons, in this new book, provides a helpful map for all who want to navigate the path of God's salvation plans revealed in the Bible.

The author constructs this map by using the Biblical Feasts as "grid references and marker posts" to help us see the "big picture" and to reach our destination. For many, the focus upon the Biblical Feasts will be a new approach in providing an overall theological structure to the Biblical narrative. For others well versed in the "*Jewish Biblical roots of faith*" this approach will be familiar, yet in all cases I am sure there will be an appreciation for the careful research undertaken by the author and for the important questions and challenges this book presents.

I think that Sammons is wise in presenting the Biblical Feasts within their Covenantal setting. This provides a helpful, and I believe an essential, context – helpful in terms of experiencing the feasts as an expression of God's ongoing faithfulness to His People, especially in terms of election, identity and mission.

Sammons also gives a very valuable "Jesus centred" focus, which reflects his understanding that Jesus is the "hermeneutical key" who unlocks the full revelation of God's character and purposes. As part of this "Jesus centred" approach, Sammons engages carefully with issues of continuity versus discontinuity within the Biblical narrative and also engages astutely with important eschatological strands. His insights are never harshly dogmatic or simplistic, but rather are carefully weighed and pastorally balanced.

All in all, this material is important. The book will reward the careful reader and it is well set out with a number of helpful graphics, detailed Biblical references and a useful list of books for additional reading, reflection and study.

I warmly commend this book to you, both for personal and group study. Happy reading and feasting!

Rev Alex Jacob
CEO, CMJ

SPECIAL NOTES

The author wishes to record his gratitude to several trusted friends who provided constructive feedback, comment and challenge to the original manuscript.

Readers should be aware that the diagrams used in this book are not drawn to scale. Most of the Moedim are day only events. In the diagrams they therefore appear 'larger' than they are. Note also that the particular events can move position slightly dependent on moon phases. However the overall 'pattern' does not change.

PART 1

SETTING THE SCENE –
THE PATTERN FOR ETERNITY

Chapter 1

PATTERN IS GOOD

Setting the Scene – Patterns

Patterns are both useful and comforting. Life is full of patterns upon which we all, to a greater or lesser extent, depend. There are 365 days in a year, unless it's a leap year. The seasons are dependable; Spring, Summer, Autumn and Winter follow in strict order. Each day the sun rises, reaches its zenith and later sets. The night sky is full of patterns that we can enjoy (subject to light pollution!) and from which we can even navigate, if our GPS system is not working properly. We just need to locate the North Star .... The phases of the moon help us to set our astronomical clocks, as well as influencing the tides of the sea. Their immutable pattern is New, Waxing Crescent, First Quarter, Waxing Gibbous, Full, Waning Gibbous, Last Quarter, Waning Crescent, New.

This book is, first and foremost, a biblical exploration and sets out the simple proposition that God also uses patterns – indeed that He wisely and graciously set those patterns in place, ultimately for our benefit and blessing. Whilst there are a number of patterns that God graciously uses, He set out His pattern for life and His pattern for relationship for the blessing of all mankind, especially through His chosen people, the Hebrews. In this book we will explore this pattern – traditionally called the Moedim[1] – and see how it speaks to us of the life, ministry and mission of Jesus. It is important to emphasise that God's "chosen people" is not limited to, nor simplistically identified with, those who happen to be Jewish – God has a plan of expansion or enlargement as He builds His chosen family. God's family was always going to be a big family! God's family is always growing, and has a place for you and me.

It is important to say, right at the outset, that this book does not see itself as an element of the "Hebrew Roots Movement" – whatever that may be! Some quite wacky ideas have emerged under that general heading, amongst which some have been well meaning but misguided, and others have been undeniably mischievous in intent. But there is a hugely important truth attached to the Hebrew Moedim, and we are not to be denied access to these truths simply because there is confusion and sometimes even misrepresentation on the matter. This book seeks to bring a little order and Jesus-focus into this subject.

We must straightaway affirm that whilst this pattern was given to *the* Chosen People – the Hebrews – God always intended that this Chosen People would be expanded or enlarged to encompass people from "every tribe and tongue".[2] So the subject of this book is not a vague and arcane matter of only limited interest, this subject speaks to every human being on the face of this planet. A large claim to make, but I trust that this book will make good on its promise.

Writers will often outline the readership to which they hope their book will appeal, as they seek to establish a rapport with those readers. There are three categories of reader that I hope will encounter this book:

- those who know *nothing* of Jesus and want a biblical introduction

- those who have been followers of Jesus for (perhaps) years and want to reinvigorate their relationship with Him

- those who sense that in some way the future is linked with Jesus, Who made it clear that He would return when the time is right

No book is written in isolation from broader influences. The whole subject of the Moedim was opened up for me through Rosemary Bamber's exhaustive Bible Study Notes contained in her book *In Time with God* (at the time of writing still widely available – see the Select Bibliography at the back of this book). The Rev Alex Jacob opened up to me the difficulties with, and inadequacies of, the two erroneous "theologies" that are now widely known and recognised as Replacement Theology and Two Covenant Theology. Alex, a personal friend (and former local minister) has explored exhaustively the correct and safe middle course between these two theological extremes and developed a nomenclature for the correct biblical course – which he calls "Enlargement Theology". Alex's book *The Case For Enlargement Theology* is likewise still widely available at the time of writing this book. Thirdly, another personal friend, Steve Maltz, is probably the man who has most determinedly opened up, at what might be called the *popular theology* level, the whole subject of the benighted influence of ancient Greek philosophy on the history of the early Christian church – an influence that still impacts, guides and arguably misleads the institutional church[3] to this very day. It is only correct that I should mention these writers, alongside the internationally renowned David Pawson, whose various Works have been regular companions on my own walk of faith for some thirty or more happy years, so that readers get a sense of "where" I am coming from.

We live in a modern age that is in many ways disconnected from reading, let alone disconnected from Jesus. I make no apology that this is a study that requires readers to engage with it at a deeper level than do many "lightweight" Christian books, and to diligently work through its premises and evidences. Unusually for this type of book, we make greater use than some readers will be used to of simple diagrams to put across and illustrate sometimes complex themes. The good news, however, is that a diligent and determined reader can, to a large extent, personalise this book and return to it from time to time to revisit old ground or to recapitulate on subjects they may have struggled with at first reading. There are various "check boxes" to help readers, literally, to check-off their progress, especially in reviewing the many Bible references that pepper this study. *Your author does not seriously expect his readers to review each and every biblical reference*, however he considers that you will get more "bang for the buck" as you do, and he suspects that you will not be disappointed in discovering that the various and numerous references do, very much, illustrate the points being made.

The Bible makes its own promise to its readers. **"My word,"** affirms God, **"will not return to me empty"** (Isaiah 55:11). In other words *any* engagement with the Bible, even at a fairly superficial level (although not with a superficial attitude!) will be rewarded by the Holy Spirit of God. If this book achieves nothing else, it would be good to know that it has encouraged readers, metaphorically speaking, to roll up their sleeves, find a quiet corner, and really dig-in to the Scriptures. As you do, I guarantee that you will not be disappointed.

Setting the Scene – The Bible

Your author recognises that most readers will approach this book with limited knowledge of the Bible – and some with absolutely no knowledge whatsoever. These readers can have confidence that in working through this book they will acquire a little 'head knowledge' along the way. This is not going to be a crash course on the Bible or on theology, but inevitably readers will pick up some understanding of the Bible as they follow the argument. In this introduction we will, however, make three simple observations about the Bible, so readers can get a clear sense of how the author approaches the subject:

* The Bible is divided into Old and New Testaments

This immediately sounds rather obscure and the author acknowledges that these titles and divisions are not altogether helpful. The Old Testament tells of the dealings of God with humans in history, and especially through His *Chosen People* – the Hebrews. The New Testament tells of God's dealings with humankind through Jesus, His Son, whom His followers called "Lord", as they acknowledged Him to have ultimate control over their lives. Old Testament and New Testament might better be thought of as "The Promise" (for the Old Testament) and "The Promise Fulfilled" for the New Testament. This at least recognises that the Old reveals God's insistent promise that He will one day send a Saviour to the world, whilst the New reveals who that Saviour is. But even these titles are not altogether helpful, as some of the promises of the Old Testament (and indeed some promises in the New Testament) are yet to be fulfilled – in the future. But, even so, try to hold on to the thought of *promise* and *promise fulfilled* as you work through this book. The idea at least provides a context in which to think about the 66 books that make up the Bible and the way the two "Testaments" stand in relation to each other. They are interconnected in very many ways – the New does not replace the Old – it confirms it. *Hand in Glove* might be a better analogy for the way these two "Testaments" relate to each other.[4]

* Just how do we read the Bible – and is it dependable anyway?
Let's just consider its dependability for a moment: in this book we do not set out to defend the Holy Scriptures as the definitive word of God. There are many good books that examine the Holy Bible in that context and no doubt someone who is genuinely interested in this subject will readily find what they need without having to look too hard. If the reader comes to this book with the objection that the Bible *is not*, or *may not be*, the sole revelation of "god" then he or she is invited simply to "park" that objection for the time being. There surely can be no great problem in looking closely at what the Scriptures have to say about God's chosen meetings (or assemblies) with His people so as to acquire a clear understanding of the argument being advanced in this book.

In a court of law, as each witness gives their testimony, a judge and jury will form an opinion as to the trustworthiness of that particular person, and the validity of the testimony they offer. The author invites the reader to adopt the same attitude towards the Bible. Readers can always "call more witnesses" at a later stage if they feel that the witness of Scripture is incomplete or invalid. The key suggestion made by this author is that a doubter holds on to his or her doubts but proceeds from this point onwards with the basic working assumption that the Scriptures *are* valid and trustworthy. If at the conclusion of this book the reader finds the testimony of Scripture is finally un-compelling, then he or she is free to take up their doubts once more. Until then, let us use the Scriptures as the primary platform from which to review what God says to us about this question of patterns and His overarching purposes displayed through the Biblical Feasts, or Moedim.

Allowing that many readers will be Westerners, then we might as well also "park" the gender issue: some may feel that reference to God as 'Him' and 'He' represents a form of gender aggression. If so, you too are simply invited to park that objection for the time being. We use those terms because the Bible uses those terms. You can always return to your objection later if you feel that the gender question remains a challenge for you personally. In the same way we use the term "mankind", not because "this is a man's world", but because the Bible uses this term and because it has a theological resonance that is (well) beyond the scope of this book. But we do affirm, for anyone who is particularly interested in this subject, that men and women are created equal, though distinct, before God – and we specifically agree with the apostle Paul who says that in God, with respect to salvation, *there is neither male nor female* (Galatians 3:28 and Colossians 3:11).

* So how do we read the Bible?
In essence the way most serious Christians read the Bible is to take the text at its plainest and simplest meaning – in other words the way the writer clearly meant the words to be read and understood. We should only read the text in another way if it is quite obvious that the writer or the context demands that it be read differently. That is the approach adopted in this book.

Setting the Scene - Outcomes
Precisely what outcome can you expect from reading this book? There are in fact several:

- It will give you a "handle" on the Moedim – those seven appointed meetings that most clearly set out the entire good news ("gospel") theme
- It will help you to see more clearly God's great plan of salvation
- It will highlight the 'topography' of the end times
- It will give you greater insight into "one new man", the reality of two that are, in some senses, in outright opposition to each other, and yet can be united eternally in Messiah Jesus
- It should help to "lock" in your mind's eye the "contours" of the life, ministry, mission and triumph of Jesus
- It should help to "unlock" the entire Bible to you and give you greater confidence in its dependability and truthfulness

The Moedim
The theme of this book is simply and straightforwardly that in giving to the Chosen People a "framework" within which to encounter Him in a formalised sense, God is doing more than "just" providing a few interesting festivals and holy convocations, or reflecting the agricultural planting and reaping seasons. Taken in aggregate, the Moedim provide a

simple and straightforward message that speaks of two profound things simultaneously:

- the life, death, mission, ministry and return of Jesus the Messiah
- God's future plans for mankind

We would add that in the Moedim we see a simple and straightforward gospel message. In our Bibles we read that the risen Lord Jesus, in the road to Emmaus encounter,[5] took two confused disciples[6] through the entire Scriptures so as to demonstrate to them "everything" about himself. Your author is of the opinion that it is likely that the structure of the Lord's "Bible study" would have been the Moedim.

We can say, then, that the Moedim provide a wonderful "framework" within which to consider all of God's works. In this book we set the scene in chapters 2 and 3, as we outline the covenant promises of God, and how they are "enlarged" to encompass all mankind. Again this is a big subject and largely beyond the scope of this study, however one excellent resource that looks in great detail at this related subject is Alex Jacob's book *The Case for Enlargement Theology* (summarised in his shorter popular title *Receive the Truth*).[7] Having set the scene on some big issues, we then explore each of the seven Moedim in part 2 of this book. The Appendices add further depth to particular subjects.

We would make one very simple observation as you work through this book. It is the Bible that is the ultimate authority on the subjects we are exploring. If the assertions of this author depart from the clear teaching of Scripture, then it is the clear teaching of Scripture that a reader should trust. This book is written with the simple prayer that its readers will emerge with a clearer knowledge of and love for the Lord Who is so wonderfully revealed in the Moedim.

Since the Moedim speak with precision about the Jewish Messiah, and arguably are solely about the Jewish Messiah, one obvious question relating to the Lord's name is: should we refer to Him by His Hebrew name or the English translation of that Hebrew name? Throughout this book we use the Hebrew word *Yeshua* and its English counterpart Jesus interchangeably. There is no particular "method" in this; the word Jesus is most often used as that is the word with which most readers will be familiar. More and more Christians are using the Lord's Hebrew name[8] in everyday discourse, so our interchangeable use seems entirely appropriate in this second decade of the twenty-first century.

Notes

[1] סדאומ – Moedim – a plural Hebrew word meaning "appointments" or "appointed times". Leviticus chapter 23 contains significant references to God's appointed times. This word is sometimes translated as, "holidays", "festivals", or "feasts" but is better understood as Divinely commanded appointments, or "holy convocations". See *Strong's* #4150. Pronounced MO eh DEEM. Plural "moedim".

[2] For illustration, see Revelation 5:9 and Revelation 7:9. This theme of blessing to all mankind is found in the earliest parts of the Bible, as we shall explore later on in this book.

[3] We make a distinction between the institutions that so often govern the various denominational churches, and what Jesus referred to as His true church; sadly, the two do not always coincide.

[4] Turn to Appendix 5 for further insights into this subject of 'Old' versus 'New'.

[5] Luke 24:13-35 and Mark 16:12-13

[6] one of whom is identified as Cleopas (Luke 24:18)

[7] See Select Bibliography.

[8] Most serious scholars, and indeed theologians, are agreed that the Lord's Hebrew name is Yeshua or Y'shua, depending on pronunciation. Some commentators have introduced variations on this and advance what they take to be 'evidences' in support of their assertions. These people often become very defensive or aggressive when their assertions are not accepted, and can be both divisive and highly legalistic in their prejudices. Your author's opinion, for what it is worth, is that these religious people should be given a wide berth by those seeking the Lord – as many of them are busily building their own private religion!

Chapter 2

COVENANT PROMISES

Setting the Scene

In the Old Testament, those Scriptures that reveal the history of the Chosen People and point towards the coming Saviour of the world – or Messiah – God unveils His great plan of Salvation. From the pages of the Old Testament we learn about the origins of this world, the origins of mankind, the origins of sin and rebellion against God, the choosing of a representative People, the special place of Israel in the unveiling of God's righteous plans. Supremely we learn through God's covenant promises to His people. "At the very heart of the love story running throughout Scripture", writes Australian author Kelvin Crombie,[1] "is the principle of covenant. Covenant is the vehicle, the arrangement (or legal channel) God has ordained in order to have relationship or communion with us, His special created beings." Crombie usefully explains that the major theme running through the Bible is God's desire for relationship with humankind. Harmony in the Garden of Eden developed into a broken relationship, as Adam and Even defied the one command that God had given to them. From the very beginning, God communed with mankind through a *legal* framework – a commandment (Genesis 2:17). That God should communicate with us through a *legal* framework should not be a great surprise to us, as God's entire created order is part of a structured and well-ordered system. God only reveals Himself and His criteria for right living through such an orderly system. As Crombie notes, "the orderly manner, or perhaps we could term it, 'the legal manner', God adopted in order to present Himself and His Kingdom principles is through the principle of covenant."[2]

The foundations for two groups of people in the world today are based upon being in a covenant relationship with God:

1. The Jewish people as a nation
2. Individuals, both Jewish and Gentile, who confess faith in, and who are in a covenant relationship with, Jesus of Nazareth

The identity of the Jewish nation is based upon the promises made by God to Abram (Abraham) which were later confirmed to his son Isaac and his grandson Jacob. Of the many promises given to Abraham, most relate to his physical descendants. And of these numerous promises, we need to note especially three:

• there would be a People from his loins
• this People would inherit a piece of land called Israel
• all families on earth would be blessed through Abraham

Each male Hebrew (Jewish) child born thereafter would be circumcised on the eighth day in a ceremony known as the *brit mila*. The Hebrew word for covenant is *brit* (pronounced b'rit). And that child is known as a *son of the covenant*. The whole identity of the Jewish people is based upon this covenant. Jewish and non-Jewish people who enter a covenant relationship with God through Jesus are partakers in this same promise. It is an amazing thought that when disciples of Jesus partake of the rite known as communion (or Holy Communion) and recite those wonderful words "This cup is the new covenant in my blood, do this as often as you drink it in remembrance of Me" (1 Corinthians 11:25) they are remembering precisely that, as individuals, they are in covenant with Jesus.

As Kelvin Crombie notes, "Covenant is not just a word, it is a real and tangible concept and is the very foundation of our identity as followers of Jesus. We only enter into the Kingdom of God because of our covenant relationship with Jesus whereupon we are then sealed with the Holy Spirit."[3] The subject of covenant, in detail, is beyond the scope of this book and interested readers should pursue their own study. Two helpful starting points are Kelvin Crombie's majestic work already cited (it extends to 340 pages and 48 digestible chapters) and a much shorter "Research Paper" published by the UK's Church's Ministry Among Jewish People (CMJ) called "Covenant and Promise

– An Analysis of Biblical Principles of Covenant – *the interaction of conditionality and promise in covenant theology*". At a mere 16 printed pages this is quite short, but is scholarly and an excellent introductory study by Frank Booth.

Your author also explored this subject in rather greater outline than he intends to here in his earlier book *Rebel Church* where he developed a "table" indicating the key five covenants of the Bible, demonstrating at a glance which are conditional promises and which are unconditional promises. This table is incorporated as Appendix 3 to this book. Whilst the Covenants are of secondary importance to our key subject of the Moedim, we can make some simple (and it is hoped, memorable) observations here. There is a sense in which covenant, like any formal agreement, must have a purpose, a direction and a destination. We depict the Bible's covenants as an arrow from left to right.[4] There are four covenants that relate to God's purposes for His chosen people (and in that term we mean both Jew and Gentile, but in differing ways). Let us consider them:

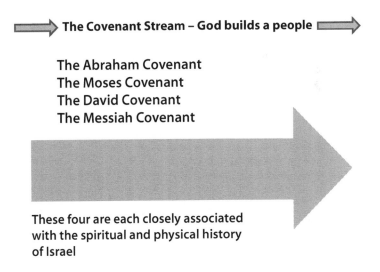

The Covenant Stream – God builds a people

The Abraham Covenant
The Moses Covenant
The David Covenant
The Messiah Covenant

These four are each closely associated with the spiritual and physical history of Israel

Through Israel God has a plan and a design that brings blessing to all mankind, whether Jew or Gentile. Each covenant is directly associated with Jesus the Messiah – but we will not fully explore that aspect in this book. We can affirm that each covenant adds progressively "finer detail" to God's overall salvation plan.

The Covenant Stream – God builds a people

The Abraham Covenant

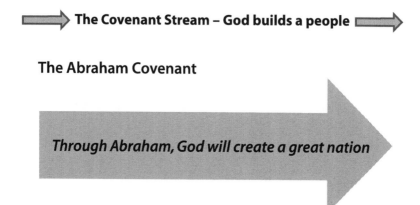

Through Abraham, God will create a great nation

**Genesis 12: 2–3; also Gen 12:7; Gen 15: 5–7
Gen 22: 16–18; Exodus 3:8; Ex 3:17; Ex 6: 6–8**

This is the foundational promise to Abraham. It is clear that the "nation" to be created will be a big nation, far bigger than the nation we today think of as Israel. Rather, we need to think of an enlarged nation encompassing people across the entire world.

I will make you into a great nation, and I will bless you; I will make your name great, and you will be a blessing. I will bless those who bless you, and whoever curses you I will curse; and all peoples on earth will be blessed through you. (Genesis 12:2-3)

The Covenant Stream – God builds a people

The Moses Covenant

The Hebrews will become a Nation of Priests, to the blessing of the entire world

Exodus 19:5–6; Exodus 20 (all); unlike the Abraham and David covenants, this one is conditional on obedience. Exodus 34:10ff sets out the conditions applicable.

By God's gracious allowance, Priests had access to God through sacrifice. They could not meet Him face to face, as it were, except and unless their sins were atoned for. The Jewish nation would become a nation of priests, but again extending across the planet.

Now if you obey me fully and keep my covenant, then out of all nations you will be my treasured possession. Although the whole earth is mine, you will be for me a kingdom of priests and a holy nation. (Exodus 19:5-6)

We need to note, straight away, that the nomenclature "the Moses Covenant" requires explanation. Some theologians take the view that the covenant expressed in Exodus 24 is "the Mosaic Covenant". That covenant, in turn, is seen as "confirming" the specific "laws" given by God to Moses in Sinai (Exodus 21 through 23) and encompasses all the other "laws" expressed in the Torah. Your author prefers to call these the Sinai Covenant. When in this book we refer to the Moses Covenant we are referring specifically to the covenant given by God in Exodus 19 - and especially verses 5 and 6. Here is the conditional promise that *if* the Israelites obey God *then* they will be for Him a Kingdom of Priests.

We should note that this covenant was also given at Sinai, and it was Moses who went up to face the Lord (verse 3) and receive the tems of this promise, so in this sense it is associated most closely with the man Moses. However some theologians call this the covenant struck with The House of Jacob, or the Jacob Covenant. When they say that they are in turn reflecting that Jacob is synonimous with Israel. That would be a more Jewish way to understand this. Readers should therefore be well aware of how this book is using the term "The Moses Covenant" and also be aware that a range of terms are in common usage.

The Covenant Stream – God builds a people

The David Covenant

God promises to David that he will, forever, have a descendent reigning upon his throne

2 Samuel 7: 13–16; see also 1 Samuel 16: 13; Also 2 Samuel 7 (all) and 2 Samuel 23:5

He is the one who will build a house for my Name, and I will establish the throne of his kingdom forever. I will be his father, and he will be my son. When he does wrong, I will punish him with a rod wielded by men, with floggings inflicted by human hands. But my love will never be taken away from him, as I took it away from Saul, whom I removed from before you. Your house and your kingdom will endure forever before me; your throne will be established forever.' (2 Samuel 7:13-16)

In the above we can see that there is a "political" dimension to the covenant relationship; there is to be a leadership provided by a King. This leadership will be reckoned through the line of King David, who will have a "successor" reigning on David's throne throughout eternity. This King will be more than "just" a King however – this is not politics as we understand it! This King will have a three-fold ministry: He will be Prophet, Priest and King, all rolled into one. Readers by now may be acquiring an insight into the identity of this prophet Who is also a priest, and Who is also a king. The term used to describe such a man is Messiah. But this Messiah will not be in any way recognisable as a "leader" in the world's mould, and that is one reason why Jesus was not universally recognised in His Own day by His Own people in first century Judea/Galilee. The identity of this Messiah is only progressively revealed though the Old Testament (or "the promise" as we suggested in the Introduction to this book):

The Covenant Stream – God builds a people

The Messiah Covenant

God points towards what will be the role and the office of Messiah

• in Jeremiah we learn what the Messiah will be
• in Ezekiel we learn how God will bring life from death
• in Isaiah we learn who this Messiah will be

"The days are coming," declares the LORD, "when I will make a new covenant with the people of Israel and with the people of Judah. It will not be like the covenant I made with their ancestors when I took them by the hand to lead them out of Egypt, because they broke my covenant, though I was a husband to them," declares the LORD. "This is the covenant I will make with the people of Israel after that time," declares the LORD. "I will put my law in their minds and write it on their hearts. I will be their God, and they will be my people. No longer will they teach their neighbor, or say to one another, 'Know the LORD,' because they will all know me, from the least of them to

the greatest," declares the LORD. "For I will forgive their wickedness and will remember their sins no more." This is what the LORD says, he who appoints the sun to shine by day, who decrees the moon and stars to shine by night, who stirs up the sea so that its waves roar — the LORD Almighty is his name: "Only if these decrees vanish from my sight," declares the LORD, "will Israel ever cease being a nation before me." This is what the LORD says: "Only if the heavens above can be measured and the foundations of the earth below be searched out will I reject all the descendants of Israel because of all they have done," declares the LORD. (Jeremiah 31:31-37)

So a new and better covenant is a part of God's Salvation plan. The "what" of the plan is expressed above. The "how" is expressed in Ezekiel chapter 37 – in its entirety. And the "who" element is expressed in Isaiah chapters 52 and 53. Readers can usefully pause at this point and read these marvellous scriptures for themselves:

Messiah (how) – Ezekiel 37 (all)

Messiah (who) – Isaiah 52:13 – 53:12

With these four covenants we can see that God has an inter-linked Salvation plan that involves a global family comprising people from every nation – adopted to be a part of God's wider, enlarged family. Within this salvation plan – to build a family that will enjoy God's blessings forever – we can begin to see how the four key covenants work together.

The Covenant Stream – God builds a people

Abraham – a mighty nation

Moses – a nation of priests

David – a mighty king Who reigns forever

Messiah – the Messiah will be a King, Who will also be a suffering servant

The covenants are each working towards a definite end point, to the incarnation of the Messiah as a human being, Who will be Prophet, Priest and King. (When we say Priest, in fact we can clarify this as not "just" any Priest: He is in fact the *High Priest*, who alone is authorised to enter into the very presence of God the Father). How does biblical Christianity relate to these covenants and the promises that they contain? We can perhaps begin to see, in a simple way, that these are different aspects of God's Salvation plan.

So which covenant is "enlarged" so as to encompass and bless all mankind? In one sense all four key covenants are enlarged to encompass all who place their faith and trust in Jesus. But we might say that "operationally" it is the Abraham covenant that is truly enlarged. To Abraham was given the promise of a mighty nation extending to the ends of the earth. Disciples of Jesus are "adopted" by God the Father to be a part of that spiritual nation, which encompasses both believing Jew and believing Gentile.

It is perhaps relatively easy to see how these covenantal promises impact the Jewish people as a Nation. It is less easy to see how they relate to those who are true disciples of Jesus – and we need to remember that this encompasses both Jewish people and non-Jewish people ("Gentiles") across this planet. It is the apostle Paul in his letter to the Roman church – and especially in its eleventh chapter – who gives the clearest picture of *how* the covenant promises work together, and how Gentiles benefit from them. Paul builds the case that the true Israelite nation are those who have been "adopted" by God as His special (chosen) people, marked out by their being given the glorious covenants (9:3). We note that Paul uses the plural – covenants – indicating that each covenant builds upon the previous one. They are to be understood as a package, to use a modern business term. Paul goes on in chapter 9 to emphasise that "not all Israel are Israel" (9:6) as he unveils the spiritual truth that some Jewish people would emphatically reject their Messiah, and some non Jewish people would accept and receive the Jewish Messiah – these too are *children of adoption* by God. It was always God's plan that His chosen people would be enlarged with members drawn from across the face of this planet!

Romans chapters 9 and 10 explore the apparent failing of the Chosen

People to respond to God's call of sacrificial love. Romans 10:10-12 provides one of the most straightforward statements of the Christian faith found in the entire Bible:

If you declare with your mouth, "Jesus is Lord," and believe in your heart that God raised him from the dead, you will be saved. For it is with your heart that you believe and are justified, and it is with your mouth that you profess your faith and are saved. As Scripture says, "Anyone who believes in him will never be put to shame."

How, then, do non-Jewish people partake of the covenant promises? In response to, and in recognition of, the rejection by the (majority of the) Jewish people, so God's gracious invitation will be extended to all mankind – everywhere on planet earth.[5]

Paul employs his *olive tree metaphor* (Romans 11:17) as a description of how this works in practice. The olive tree in this context is a metaphor for Israel.[6] Paul reminds the Gentiles that it is because of Israel's rejection of Messiah that the invitation is extended to them (11:11) and that this "loss" for the Jewish nation results in "riches" for the Gentile nations (11:12). The Jewish rejection results in "reconciliation for the world" (11:15). It is in verse 17 that the "mechanics" of this becomes apparent; if some of the cultivated olive tree branches have been broken off, this has been done to make room for "wild olive" branches to be grafted in. There is a warning for Gentile believers in this too: they should not be proud and think that in some way they have "replaced" the Jews in God's affections. These proud Christians are reminded of two things: firstly, the root supports them, they do not support the root (11:18). Secondly, God may break them away from the olive tree in precisely the same way He broke off the cultivated olive branches (11:21) if, like Israel, they fall into the world's way of thinking and behaving. Some Christians dispute whether Paul's olive tree metaphor is a reference to Israel, a surprising assertion given that the context of Romans chapters 9 through 11 is all about God's ongoing purposes for His true Chosen People. They claim that Believers are to be rooted in Jesus, not into Israel. They rather miss the point, however: the Lord Jesus does, indeed, command that we must be rooted in Him and the metaphor He chooses is the vine [John 15:1-6

]. When Paul employs the metaphor of the olive tree in the context of Romans chapter 11 it is clear from the immediate context and the entire discourse of Romans chapters 9-11 that the relationship of the Gentile believer to God's true Israel is the subject that is being explored.

Disciples of Jesus, then, are grafted into the covenantal promises. If they happen to be ethnically Jewish their journey to salvation is precisely the same as that of a non-Jew – they must repent and believe. To "repent" means to turn away from all sin; to "believe" means to trust in the achievement of Jesus at Golgotha through the crucifixion *and* to live a righteous life. Belief is never mere mental assent to the truth of Jesus – it is a belief that acts; it is a belief that proves itself in action.

We might then ask: at what point in history did this grafting-in actually happen? We can say that the in-grafting became possible at the point of the resurrection, when the Lord arose from death. He had proved his Lordship even over death, He had proved the claims He made about Himself during His three year ministry leading up to His crucifixion, and He had proved that God's promises are to be trusted. At this point and from then on, all who place their faith in the Jewish Messiah Jesus are grafted in as wild olive shoots (yes, in reality even if they are ethnically Jewish – like people everywhere they have sinned and fallen short of the glory of God,[7] and so need to be reconnected to those covenantal promises). We can characterise this definite point in history in the simple diagram below:

⟹ The Covenant Stream – God builds a people ⟹

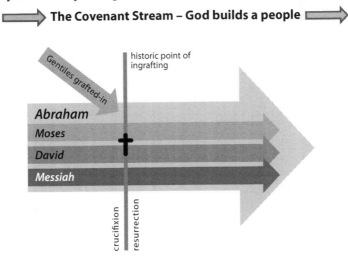

Gentiles grafted-in

historic point of ingrafting

Abraham

Moses

David

Messiah

crucifixion

resurrection

All of history, in a very real sense, had been leading up to this point. The wedding invitation, if you like, is now issued to everyone on earth. The wonderful covenant promises are now available to all. Whilst we do not want to get too bogged down in theological detail, we can make some simple supportive observations. The first is that, at this point of in-grafting, there was a definite reconfiguration of the potential relationship of individual people with their God. There was a clear break with the past. No longer do people have to become Jewish in order to be blessed by these covenant promises. Once they place their faith in the Jewish Messiah they have, in a sense, become honorary Jews and are now beneficiaries of all the covenantal promises. Prior to this point a person had to become a Jew in order to follow the God of the Jews. This is no longer the case. Historically, we can see that God foreknew the events that would follow the resurrection. Soon enough, the Second Temple in Jerusalem would be laid waste and the Levitical priesthood would be obliterated forever. Second Temple Judaism would morph into Rabbinical Judaism, and would lose sight of the Messianic promises. So there was a definite *point of departure* from the past in the resurrection event.

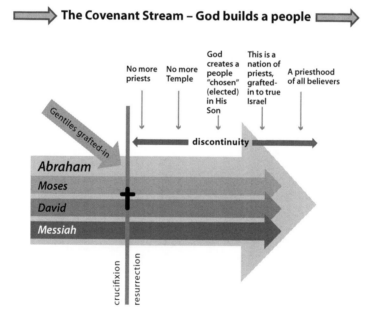

As this diagram summarises, there is now no longer a separate "priesthood" because God's family is *a priesthood of all believers*.[8] By allowing the destruction of the Second Temple and the loss of the Levitical priesthood, God simply underlined the reality of this discontinuity with the past. For each of the points indicated above we could incorporate a separate written section to explore the full implications, but we will not over-burden our book in this way. We need to note, however, that there is a degree of continuity with the past. Some Christians make a song-and-a-dance (literally!) about discontinuity, but refuse to acknowledge continuity with God's covenantal promises, especially as it relates to Israel. Rather they seek to "spiritualise" them and say that the covenant promises are somehow completed in "the church". This unbiblical idea effectively – and I choose my words advisedly and carefully – makes God out to be a liar, to say that the promises that He plainly and straightforwardly gave, He later abrogated. This is the error known as "Replacement Theology" – a subject, again, rather beyond the scope of this book. Readers should, at least, be aware of this error and be alert to it. In this early twenty-first century period, Replacement Theology is emerging as a key fault-line in theology and praxis amongst those who call themselves "Christian".

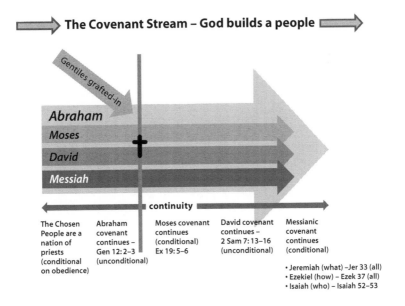

So we see, in the foregoing, that there is a degree of continuity with the Old Testament promises – and we need to hold this continuity in holy tension with the discontinuity that we considered earlier. They are, if you like, two sides of the same coin.

More detail on this can be found in Appendix 3. The simple point we need to bear in mind is that God's covenantal promises are 100% dependable. In the same way that there is a pattern in the Moedim, so there is a pattern in the covenants. They are consistent. They are incremental. They are "legal" and have "legal" force. They build towards an overarching promise that Jesus will successfully assemble for Himself a family of those who truly love Him. The relationship of this family to its Lord is likened to a marriage in the Bible. In the Old Testament, God is said to be married to Israel. In the New Testament, Jesus is the bridegroom of His bride – the family of all those who repent of sin and instead place their faith and trust in Him. Entry into this (multi-ethnic) family is identical for all: it is through faith and by grace.

Notes
[1] *In Covenant With Jesus*, 2012, ISBN 978098763008. Available via CMJ in the UK.
[2] Op cit, p 1
[3] Op cit, p 3
[4] There is no particular significance in this. It might equally have been depicted from right to left, but to Western readers in particular, the left to right sequence implies temporal progression, and this is precisely what is implied here in regard to the covenants.
[5] Jesus Himself alludes to this extended invitation in the parable of the King's marriage feast – see Matthew 22:1-14. Those outside the invited guest list, will receive invitations and will take up their place ....
[6] In Jeremiah 11:16-17, Israel is called a "green olive tree" that is fair, and of goodly fruit, but is warned that for its idolatry its branches will be broken off. Could this be one of those great coincidences in the Bible? Romans 11:16-17 is mirrored precisely in Jeremiah 11:16-17. Yet it would not be until more than a thousand years after the Bible was written that chapter and verse numbers were added!
[7] Romans 3:23
[8] 1 Peter 2:5

Chapter 3

APPOINTED TIMES

Leviticus 23

The Bible portion that is central to this whole book is Leviticus chapter 23. The first two books of the Bible are very obviously strong on character and narrative – they are indeed *a great read*. If at first we don't see that there is also much to be learnt from Leviticus then we simply need to dig more deeply! It concerns the priestly 'tribe' of Israel and its role in the nation. It contains regulations for worship and religious ceremony. It contains regulations for the priests who were responsible for carrying out these instructions. The book of Leviticus, plainly, derives its name from the priestly tribe of the Levites. The main theme of the book, and one that is perhaps obscured by its vast detail, is the holiness of God and the ways in which His people were to worship Him, and to live in such a way as to maintain their relationship with Him. There is very little narrative in Leviticus, rather it tends to be seen as being simply a list of rules and regulations. For many people today it seems almost irrelevant. We are inclined to ask "what has this got to do with me?" If a disciple of Jesus knows anything, it is likely that they know that the detailed rules and regulations of the "Laws of Moses" no longer apply, so whilst we honour the book as part of Scripture, Leviticus seems to concern matters that are mainly no longer relevant. The kindest thing that (some) will say about Leviticus is that it helps us to see in context the need for holy living and the holiness of God. And yet there are many quotations from Leviticus in the New Testament. The best known words from the book are probably found in 19:18 "**love your neighbour as you love yourself**", and of course the Lord Jesus Himself quoted this more than once.

This book is not a study of Leviticus. If anyone wants a really good and readable introduction to Leviticus, then David Pawson's excellent *Unlocking the Bible*[1] contains a brilliant and easy to read review. But let us for one moment consider its structure:

Laws about offerings and sacrifices	1:1 – 7:38
Ordination of Aaron and his sons as priests	8:1 – 10:20
Laws about ritual cleanness and uncleanness	11:1 – 15:33
The Day of Atonement	16:1–34
Laws about holiness in life and worship	17:1 – 27:34

Clearly our interest is in the fifth section. God gave to Moses specific regulations for the worshipful year, when He commanded that the people of Israel were to *gather* together for worship. Note that word gather! This is about corporate worship and responding to God in community. In Leviticus 23:3 God reiterates the fourth of what we all call The Ten Commandments; in Exodus 20:8 God had commanded that the people should observe the Sabbath and keep it holy. In this context 'holy' means set apart specifically for worship of the Lord. That command is repeated virtually word for word in Leviticus. Because of this, and the fact that it comes immediately before the seven Moedim, some commentators will speak of eight Moedim and incorporate the weekly Sabbath into this pattern of worship. Their keenness and enthusiasm is commendable, but they are incorrect. The Sabbath is for all time and for all peoples. It is a command and a pattern that is given for the blessing of the whole of humanity, but, unlike the seven Moedim it does not speak in the same way of the life, death, resurrection and completed mission of Jesus. It is rightly said that Jesus is our "Sabbath rest"[2] if we are His true disciples; however it is not an exaggeration to say that an entire theology book could be devoted just to this wonderful subject. Sabbath is of a different order to the Moedim and so we largely ignore it in this book, not because it is unimportant (far from it) but because it is simply a hugely different subject.[3] So there are seven, not eight Moedim.

The fact that there are seven Moedim is significant in itself. The number seven in the Bible is always an indication of completion and of perfection. When God says something seven times we should sit up and listen! The fact of the seven Moedim means that God has provided a complete and a perfect message within them. There is nothing to be added – and nothing to be subtracted. Readers may want to pause at this point and read Appendix 4 "The Magnificent Seven", which is a brief exploration of the number seven as found in our Bibles.

In the account of the creation event (or perhaps we should say *the creation events* [plural] as they are divided up into six separate "days"), we read that on the fourth day God issued this command: **"Let there be lights in the vault of the sky to separate the day from the night, and let them serve as signs to mark sacred times, and days and years, and let them be lights in the vault of the sky to give light on the earth." And it was so. God made two great lights – the greater light to govern the day and the lesser light to govern the night. He also made the stars. God set them in the vault of the sky to give light on the earth, to govern the day and the night, and to separate light from darkness. And God saw that it was good** (Genesis 1:14-18). We are perhaps so familiar with the description of the creation events that we can miss the important detail. In the quotation above we see twice that the purpose of the sun and moon are to give light – and certainly we know that the sun especially makes possible photosynthesis and enables life on earth as we understand it. But notice that there is an important (vital?) sub-clause contained in the command. Let us repeat it: **let them serve as signs to mark sacred times, and days and years** (verse 14). The purpose of the moon, in particular, seems to be to enable the setting aside of religious festivals with absolute precision.[4] Of course, whether those moon-based 'religious' ceremonies are of God is another matter entirely. We note with sorrow mankind's historic propensity to worship the moon (with all that this entails) rather than to use it simply as a 'clock' to measure times and seasons. It is rightly said that where God establishes a pattern, the devil is not far behind to establish a rival, diabolical, pattern. The sun, moon and stars should lift our thoughts to the God of Creation; but too often they become objects of veneration as people decide, instead, to worship them.[5] We need, then, to note that there is a purpose for the moon in God's economy beyond just shifting the tides around!

The calendar that the Bible uses is the lunar calendar. The "year" that the Bible marks is the agricultural year and is based on the reality of harvests. So we can begin to "plot" graphically how the Biblical year looks, by comparing it with the 'solar' year – the year based on the sun. We all think, naturally, of a twelve month cycle beginning in January. That is the solar year, and from a biblical perspective it is also the pagan year!

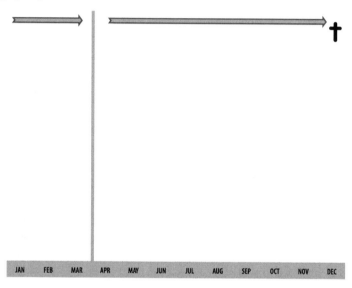

At this point we can make a simple diagram to 'plot' the thoughts above. A calendar year can be viewed in more than one way. The normal "western" year happens to reflect the so-called Gregorian Calendar which begins in January and ends in December. Whilst it may be relatively unimportant, it is worth noting that this Gregorian year also – in a very real sense – reflects a Pagan year, as each of the names of the months corresponds to a Pagan (Roman) "god". Certainly God wants us to have nothing to do with Paganism, yet God's children are obliged to live within the system common to mankind's various cultures. We can reflect, as well, that every religion and culture has its own calendar, usually based on lunisolar principles, but with notable variations. God's calendar for His Chosen People would, in practice, have many competitors! Unlike the Pagan calendars, however, the Hebrew calendar represents two unique things:

- it speaks of the life death resurrection and completed mission of one Man
- it speaks of the history – and especially of the future – of the whole of mankind

So in the diagram above we can see at a simplistic level two things: firstly the normal Gregorian calendar of twelve months along the bottom horizontal line, and secondly a vertical line between March and April that signals the beginning of the Hebrew agricultural year. On this basic 'template' we can "plot" the key events of the Hebrew calendar, as measured from God's perspective.

Times and Seasons

To follow God's pattern for life in the annual calendar, as set out in Leviticus 23, we need to use the same calendar, a lunar calendar. In this each month begins when the new moon appears in the night sky, and each 'day' begins at nightfall (Genesis 1:15). God 'appointed the moon for seasons' (Psalm 104:19)[6] so all the Biblical Feasts happen on days set by the lunar calendar. Is the Biblical calendar still important to God, or has it been 'replaced' in some way? Since the Biblical Feasts mark out the "high points" of God's redemptive purposes and also express God's view of the history of mankind, it is superfluous to ask if His calendar and His appointed festivals are still important. Rather, we should be asking *how do they speak to us today*? The Lord Jesus died on the 'Feast of Passover' and was raised from the dead on the 'Feast of First Fruits'. The Holy Spirit was poured out at the 'Latter First Fruits'[7] as the inauguration of the time of the New Covenant, when God's Spirit would be poured into the lives of Jesus' disciples. We can say with certainty that Jesus fulfilled the prophetic meaning of these 'Feasts' on the actual days that they occurred.

The Biblical feasts, as given to Moses in Leviticus 23 (and re-emphasised with minor variations in Exodus 12, Numbers 28-29 and Deuteronomy 16) are called in Hebrew "Moedim" which means "appointed times".

These were the times appointed by God for a special revelation to the whole of mankind, and for something specific to be done. God graciously gave to the Hebrew people precise instructions about what should happen at these 'holy convocations', as they are sometimes called. This was so that He could reveal truths about Himself and His plan to bring people into His Kingdom, not only from Israel but from every tribe and tongue.[8]

These Moedim are sometimes referred to as the biblical feasts or festivals, as a sort of shorthand title. In contemporary usage "festival" usually refers to activities over a period of time whilst "feast" indicates one part of the celebration, often a meal. In religious usage, both modern and ancient, these two words tend to be used quite interchangeably. The Jews used the word Moed ("assembly" or "convocation") and *hag*[9] for their important celebrations. Feasts of a more private nature were called *mishteh*. Perhaps confusingly, the majority of English language translations of the Bible do not differentiate between these words. The more recent One New Man Bible (2015) tends to use the modern Hebrew equivalent for individual Moeds, so it is very clear which Moed is being referred to. Appendix 2 to this book lists, in tabular form, the various names in common usage today.

The seven Moedim take place in two clusters. The first three Moedim occur in the spring, the fourth in the early summer and the final three in the autumn. At His first incarnation Jesus fulfilled the symbolic message of the spring feasts, and He fulfilled them on the precise days preordained by God the Father. We know what those days were, even if we debate the precise year in which they occurred! The symbolism of the autumn Moedim has yet to be fulfilled in their entirety. They point to the future. In John 7:37-39 as Jesus spoke at the festival of Tabernacles He promised "streams of life giving water" to those who come to Him, Jesus, to "drink". As John writes, this was an allusion to the gift of the Holy Spirit, which all Believers freely receive. This reference to 'living water' reflects Zechariah 14:8 which hints at the second coming of Messiah, and in turn this is mirrored in Revelation 22:1-2, which speaks of the future when streams of "living water" will flow from the throne of the lamb.

Rosemary Bamber, in her book *In Time With God*,[10] comments that Zechariah 14 connects the Feast of Tabernacles to the future rule and reign of Messiah on earth. She observes that the Moedim in the biblical calendar represent a "time-line of history", which simultaneously connects to the natural seasons and harvests in the physical land of Israel, so history and the seasons are connected. The beginning of this time-line concerns God's plan to redeem (buy-back) and save our souls – through the perfect sacrifice of Jesus who takes away our sins and redeems us back to God. This act is represented in the first three feasts of spring. After this, through the spring and early summer, as the barley and wheat harvests are gathered in Israel, we have the growth of the 'redeemed congregation' – broadly, in modern language, the church. We note how Jesus told His disciples to take a good look and to see – not the harvest to come in four months time – but to recognise that the harvest fields were *already* "white" and ready for harvest (John 4:35 and Luke 10:2). The hot months of summer represent for us the time of the predominantly Gentile church. In the seventh month we reach the autumn feasts where the focus turns to the conclusion of "the time of the Gentiles" (Luke 21:24), to God's final purposes amongst the Jews, and to Jesus' second coming. The key themes revealed through the Moedim, then, are (1) God's plan of redemption (2) the Kingdom of God which has room both for Jews and for Gentiles, and (3) the preparation of Jesus' "bride" from amongst all the nations.

The Jewish year reflects the seasons in Israel. It is to a large extent an agricultural year in the physical realm. Yet it is also a theological year in the spiritual realm. The year begins with Jesus the Lamb of God who fulfils the symbolism of the Lamb at the spring "Feast of Passover". It moves on to the linked Moedim of "Unleavened Bread", which the Israelites were to eat for a period of seven days. The lack of leaven is a symbol of sinlessness as we shall see later in this book. Jesus is the sinless Saviour. The Moedim of "First Fruits" reflects the joy of the early harvest – and the first fruit in the Kingdom of God is the risen Lord Jesus! He is the FIRST to be raised from death, but certainly not the last! And so the spring festivals are concluded. The festival of "Latter First Fruits" (*Shavuot* in Hebrew) expresses joy at the anticipated later harvest. There is more than one legitimate way of understanding "Latter First Fruits", but the obvious way is to see these 'fruits' as being all those who place their trust and faith in the Jewish Messiah down through history until

He returns. In the autumn we reach the final cluster of three Moedim. "Trumpets" reflects the second coming of Messiah (naturally, at the end of the harvest), the announcement of which will be by the blast of shofarim (trumpets). "Atonement" reflects the reality of forgiveness and new life. Finally, "Tabernacles" is the joyful truth that Jesus and His disciples live in community forever, as He literally "tabernacles" with us. All this we will explore in greater detail in Part 2 of this book.

We can summarise these thoughts graphically:

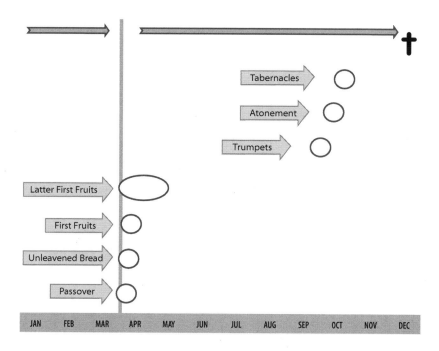

This is the pattern that we use throughout this book. It is important to note that it is not drawn to scale! Hopefully it helps to "fix" the Moedim in our mind's eye. Beyond knowing the approximate "position" of the feasts, how they develop and the gap that sits between them (something that is important and which we will explore in chapter 8) we can precisely state their dates, as we see in this graph:

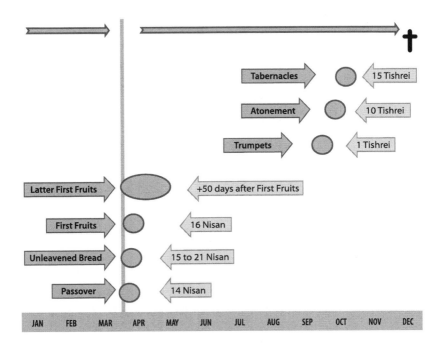

Here we are compelled to touch upon a sensitive subject: just how important are the precise days? We know when they fall each year with absolute precision. So should we feel obliged to "mark" or "observe" them today? There are some people who would say emphatically 'yes' and that any other approach in life is in some way insulting to God Who has given us such precise instructions. But this is pure legalism, and the people who hold this view will often insist upon the marking of Jewish dietary laws, Shabbat observance and so on. If they claim to be "Christians" then such legalism is in stark defiance of Paul's clear instruction to the Roman church where these matters had been encountered and debated. Paul was crystal clear, and we have no licence to disregard what he said:

One person considers one day more sacred than another; another considers every day alike. Each of them should be fully convinced in

their own mind. Whoever regards one day as special does so to the Lord. Whoever eats meat does so to the Lord, for they give thanks to God; and whoever abstains does so to the Lord and gives thanks to God. For none of us lives for ourselves alone, and none of us dies for ourselves alone. If we live, we live for the Lord; and if we die, we die for the Lord. So, whether we live or die, we belong to the Lord. For this very reason, Christ died and returned to life so that he might be the Lord of both the dead and the living. You, then, why do you judge your brother or sister? Or why do you treat them with contempt? For we will all stand before God's judgment seat. It is written: " 'As surely as I live,' says the Lord, 'every knee will bow before me; every tongue will acknowledge God.' " So then, each of us will give an account of ourselves to God. (Romans 14:5-12)

Our Christian life is not bound up with "observance" of religious ceremonies. Anyone who purports to judge another on the basis of such performance is – I am sorry to say this – probably not a true Christian in the first place. Rather they are people who are interested in external observances, in preference to internal renewal in Messiah Jesus. But with that powerful and blunt caveat, and an acknowledgement that the Christian life is never a life about slavish "performance" of externals, I would ask the question: why not observe and mark this biblical Moedim cycle which is so focused on the life, death, resurrection and completed ministry of Messiah Jesus? Not to mention the "hot summer" period that is the life of the true Church until Jesus returns. Why not be Jesus-focused throughout the year? Rather than demanding a slavish compulsion to follow Levitical details, surely the Moedim provide a wonderful opportunity to worship Jesus precisely as God has graciously revealed His mission and ministry to us all?

Beginning with Moses
Many Christians, as they consider the events immediately after Jesus' resurrection from death, are struck by the Emmaus Road encounter. This is recorded for us in detail in Luke 24:13-35 (and briefly in Mark 16:12-13). Two of Jesus' disciples were walking between Jerusalem and Emmaus and encountered a stranger on the road. As they walked

44

together they discussed the recent crucifixion event and all that it implied. The stranger, Who was in fact the risen Lord Jesus – yet was unrecognised as such – then explained to the two travellers precisely what had transpired. The record is quite clear that the stranger explained all this (verse 27) "beginning at Moses". But not before having labelled them bluntly as "foolish and slow in heart to believe"! I am sure that today many Christians must think to themselves, what a fascinating discourse this must have been, especially as Jesus led these two travellers through the Old Testament scriptures and explained to them "all" concerning Himself. Mark that: Jesus did not give them a summary, or a potted history. He explained to them "all" that was said about Himself throughout the Old Testament Scriptures.

The Good News Bible usefully paraphrases verse 27 as "Jesus explained to them what was said about himself in all the scriptures, beginning with the books of Moses and the writings of all the prophets". Wow! This must have been a wonderful Bible study! We can only conjecture at what structure this study might have taken, but undoubtedly the Moedim would have provided a useful framework to introduce supplementary scriptures such as (for example) Isaiah chapter 53 which speaks so directly of the crucifixion of the suffering servant. In fact it is difficult to think of an alternative framework that would straightforwardly take these disciples through the crucifixion, which had happened just a few days earlier, and its eternal meaning, and from thence into the future of mankind. We should note in this regard that the meeting on the road to Emmaus took place just after the end of the Moed of "Unleavened Bread", and the bread that Jesus broke at the meal table (verse 30) might therefore have been unleavened bread! It was literally at the breaking of this bread that the two disciples recognised Jesus (verse 31).

At its most straightforward, we can summarise the seven Moedim in this way:

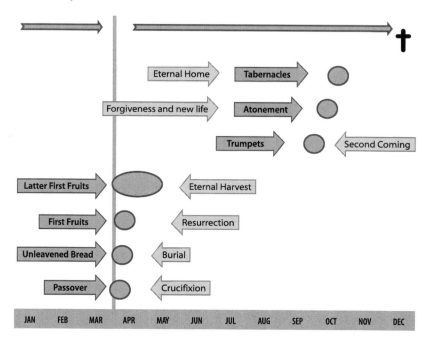

Note in the diagram above that the darker arrows provide the names of the Moedim in their most common English form. The lighter arrows speak of the "Christology" associated with each of the Moedim; in other words, the key elements of Jesus' life, death, resurrection, ministry and His future consummation of all things. This pattern is straightforward and simple – and it is precisely as God gave it in Leviticus chapter 23. Part 2 of this book will help us to explore each Moed in order, but for now we remark only how simple the pattern is. Once we have this pattern "locked" in our mind's eye, it is relatively straightforward to think about the mission of the Lord Jesus. Why the institutional church has largely ignored this pattern is, perhaps, the subject for another book. Your author can find no compelling or acceptable "reason" for this ignoring (ignorance?), but the most likely explanation is that the early church embarked upon a determined plan during the first centuries of the *Christian Era* to "de-Judaise" the early church. We remember that the

Moedim were seen as being Jewish festivals, and the State-empowered church after the time of the Emperor Constantine wanted to stamp its own mark upon their newly adopted religion.[11]

This raises more difficult questions. Again, these are questions that many church-attending Christians are reluctant to acknowledge, let alone to confront. Does the church's ecclesiastical year serve to highlight, or to obscure, the truth about the Lord Jesus? We can plot easily how the institutional church's year tends to overwrite the Moedim.

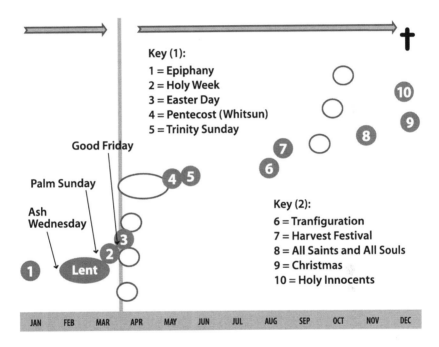

The above festivals were never commanded by God. There is no scriptural evidence that God had in mind to replace or overwrite His commanded Moedim with a new batch of festivals. So we are entitled to ask: "Where did they come from and who authorised them?" We note that the festivals plotted on the graph above represent a mere token when, for example, they are added to the literally hundreds of "saints' days" and other ephemera introduced by the institutional church. If an average Christian was asked *which is the most important Christian festival in the Christian calendar*, it is likely that most would say "Easter", and then they might add that this is because it marks the resurrection and new life in Jesus. Yet few are aware that "Easter" emerges from a pagan festival. So we need to ask ourselves an uncomfortable question: is it in any way right or justifiable that the death and resurrection of Jesus is marked by the use of a pagan feast dedicated to a fertility goddess named **Ēostre** (from which we get our word "Easter")?

We note that some Christians who are aware of this difficulty have substituted, in recent years, the term "resurrection day" to avoid, as they see it, being tarnished with a pagan festival. However we must observe that this, also, is not commanded by God anywhere – and indeed *it has been invented precisely to avoid recognition of the festival of First Fruits*, when the Lord was resurrected from death – and precisely when God said that He would raise His Son. I would gently challenge my readers: just how comfortable are you with "Easter" as your most important festival of the year?

Let us just summarise what we have explored in this Part 1 of our book, so far, and make a few assertions that we trust the remainder of the book will justify and reinforce:

- The Moedim are the gospel in outline.
- God's eternal purposes for mankind are set out in a simple pattern
- What we might call "The Jesus Plan" has been clearly in evidence for 4,000 years. Strangely, this Jesus plan has been largely ignored by the institutional church down through its history.
- The Jesus Plan 'kills two birds with one stone': (a) it details God's Salvation purposes with absolute precision – even down to our knowledge of specific days; and (b) it shows to us the relationship of two epochs, being (firstly) the era of the Christian church from the time of the crucifixion, and (secondly) the Kingdom age yet to come.
- The future is secure – the Moedim tell us about the return of Jesus.
- The future is certain – just as the first four Moedim have occurred as prophesied, so will the final three.
- We can hardly call the Moedim "new wine", as they have been in existence for nearly 4000 years. But Jesus did state quite categorically that His new wine will never be placed into old wineskins. If there is to be a rediscovery of the Moedim amongst ordinary Christians, will

this be poured into the brittle old wineskins that are the institutional church, or will the Lord Jesus create new structures – possibly even non-institutional structures, that will accommodate and expound this ancient truth for the modern day?

- The Moedim provide a 'natural' pattern for life, both for the individual believer and for the history of the Bride of Christ
- The Moedim provide a useful template for preaching the gospel to fields that are yet "white unto harvest" in the lovely words of the older King James version of the Bible.[12]

As the Passover is central to the life and ministry of Jesus, we will introduce this theme in the next chapter, before we turn to look at the Moedim, in sequence, within Part 2 of this book.

Notes

[1] *Unlocking the Bible – A Unique Overview of the Whole Bible*, Harper Collins 2015 ISBN 9780007166664 – at time of writing this book available for less than £15 in the UK!

[2] Hebrews chapter 4 is the definitive passage regarding Jesus as our Sabbath rest. The writer to the Hebrews pleads with his readers to "enter in" to the Sabbath rest provided by Messiah Jesus. After three chapters of reminding them that Jesus is superior to the angels and that He is our Apostle and High Priest, he pleads with them to not harden their hearts against Jesus, as their fathers hardened their hearts against the Lord in the wilderness. Because of their unbelief, God denied that generation access to the Holy Land, saying, "They shall not enter into My rest" (Hebrews 3:11). In the same way, the writer to the Hebrews begs his readers not to make the same mistake by rejecting God's Sabbath rest in their Messiah. "There remains, then, a Sabbath-rest for the people of God; for anyone who enters God's rest also rests from his own work, just as God did from his. Let us, therefore, make every effort to enter that rest, so that no one will fall by following their example of disobedience" (Hebrews 4:9–11).

[3] Some Christians choose voluntarily to mark Sabbath (the Jewish Shabbat) in preference to Sunday. There seems no intrinsic reason why this pattern should not be adopted *providing* it is not seen as being a Law, and something upon which our salvation is thought to depend. The Bible makes specific provision in Romans 14:5 for freedom of conscience in this area, which can otherwise become divisive and controversial.

[4] The Good News Translation helpfully renders this: "and to show the time when days, years and religious festivals begin". Whilst this is a paraphrase, it captures the "legal" reality precisely.

[5] Astrological religions create their own "pattern" in history. An interesting and useful study of what are called "the Babylonian mystery religions" is I A Sadler's *Mystery, Babylon The Great*. It provides a number of valuable insights into false religions and their interconnectedness. Unfortunately the book is difficult to get hold of as it was published privately.

[6] In the Good News Translation this is: "You created the moon to mark the months", and in the New International Version it is "the moon marks off the seasons". The One New Man Bible reflects: "He appointed the moon for seasons".
[7] The Christian church calls this, perhaps unhelpfully, "Pentecost".
[8] Revelation 5:9 and Revelation 7:9.
[9] The term *hag* indicates a festival usually observed by some sort of pilgrimage.
[10] See Select Bibliography.
[11] Would it be putting it too strongly to say "newly nationalised religion", in view of the Roman State's sponsorship from the time of Constantine?
[12] John 4:35

Chapter 4

PASSOVER FOR PROMOTION

A Chosen People

Most of us will be passed over at some time in our lives! If we are no good at sports at school, then in the PE lesson,[1] when it comes to choosing who will be in the sports team, and the 'captain' chooses his or her team mates, they will pass over the weakest and less capable candidates, focusing first on those team members who will, most likely, bring success on the sports field! The "duds" get selected only when all the capable ones have already found their place – it can be a slightly humiliating experience! The same is often true in working life. Many will "go" for a promotion interview, only to find themselves passed over as someone else is selected. This chapter argues, however, that there is a far more fundamental way in which, not only do we need to be passed over, but that indeed we should rejoice that this Passover is available to us. The Bible uniquely tells us that we *must* be passed over, not for promotion, but for eternal salvation. So how does this 'work'? The whole Bible, the whole of God's redemptive plan, leads up to this point of being passed over. Let's dig into this ....

When the children of Israel were in slavery in Egypt, probably in the Middle Bronze Age and approximately between the years 1998BC to 1598BC, coinciding with the Hyksos Dynasty of Pharaohs,[2] they were kept as slaves. We should note there is some debate among scholars and theologians as to when/where/which dynasties were involved. These details are not of particular interest for the purpose of this chapter. Extended slavery in Egypt was foretold [Genesis 15:13], and this was foretold in the context of the granting of the lands of Israel to the nation of Israel [Genesis 15:18-21]. Pharaoh had to be compelled to release the Hebrews, as we read in Exodus 3:7 through 12:51. The final event, however, that forced his hand – the proverbial straw that broke this camel's back – was the plague on the firstborn (Exodus 11:4-10). The Israelites were to avoid the outworking of this 'plague' by daubing on their door frames the blood of a slaughtered lamb, and in preparation for the flight from Egypt, the slaves were to eat a hasty meal which is today celebrated as Passover. God was clear what would happen – Genesis 11:1.

The Bible uniquely teaches that we must be passed over, not for promotion but for Salvation. [1 Corinthians 5:7; John 13:1 (actually all of John chapters 13 through 17 is relevant background, in the context of what we call "the last supper"); 1 John 2:2; 1 Peter 3:18; John 10:17]. These texts emphasise the sacrificial nature of the Messiah's ultimate act – going on our behalf to the Cross. We can fairly say that the whole Bible, and the whole of God's redemptive plan, leads up to this point of Passover. Let us fill in some details on this epoch making event....

From where did the feast (or Moed) of Passover emerge? We recall a few simple facts:

> For 400 years the children of Israel were in a foreign land, in slavery, and under hard task-masters.

> The slavery they suffered was real and there was a desperate need to end it. In fact the slavery of Israel and its subsequent abolition was specifically foretold to Abraham [Genesis 15:13 – see also Acts 7:6 in this regard].

The titanic struggle between the devil (and his proxy, Pharaoh) and Almighty God (and His proxy, Moses) is the subject matter of Exodus chapters 3 through 13. This is one of the key themes of the entire Bible. Our word "Passover" emerges from the Hebrew verb *pesach*, which signifies to pass, to leap, or to skip over. God gave the name Passover to the Moed that He inaugurated just prior to the permanent exodus of the people of Israel from their cruel bondage in Egypt. On the night preceding their escape, the angel of the Lord passed through Egypt and made good on God's promise to destroy all the first-born that were not marked with the sign of blood. The angel passed over all those Israelite households that had daubed the sign of blood outside their houses. Plainly this was an act of faith on their part, but it was an act of faith that God honoured – as He had promised to do. The feast of Passover was to be observed for seven days, according to the more detailed instructions given in Deuteronomy 16:1–8; God had already instructed that this Passover Moed would be a permanent, all-time fixture for His *chosen people* (specifically Exodus 12:14). Believers in Jesus are not obliged to observe "rules" (e.g. Genesis 12:43-49) but rather are to marvel at what God has done for us in His *Passover Lamb* – Jesus our Lord. Christians, too, have a huge stake in the Passover! Passover is the perfect "type" of the penal substitution of Messiah Jesus for His people – first for the Jew, and then for the Gentile (Romans 1:16). There is an old and a very true saying that "Jesus rescues us from the Egypt of sin, and takes us to the promised land of salvation."

What a joy is this Passover! Every human being *truly* wants and needs to be passed over – for promotion to Glory:

> ➢ promotion from slave to free [Galatians 5:1]

> ➢ promotion from "heathen" to the chosen people of God [Galatians 3:7 and 3:29; Romans 2:28-29; Romans 9:6-8]

> ➢ promotion from death to life [John 5:24; Ephesians 2:1-6]

> ➢ promotion to a mansion! [John 14:2 – this comes out best in the old King James Version, but the idea is common throughout the various translations – there is a special place in God's kingdom just for you!]

> ➢ promotion to a family [Romans 9:8; 1 John 3:1-2]

> ➢ promotion to a friend of Jesus [John 15:15]

These wonderful blessings arise directly from being passed over through the forgiveness of God the Father, "earned" by the sacrificial act of Jesus, God the Son. Passover was the number one mission of Jesus! What is the proof that all these amazing claims are true? The irrefutable proof is the empty tomb and the risen Saviour! It is well beyond the scope of this book to explore in detail the glory of the resurrection, and many competent writers and historians have done this more than adequately down through the centuries. It only remains to remind readers of 1 Corinthians 15 (all), and especially verse 2.

Christians are, first and foremost, the Passover people![3]

Jesus

Jesus is, of course, *the* Passover Lamb. The night before His crucifixion, precisely what sort of meal did He consume?

> ➤ a "communion"?

> ➤ a "last supper"?

> ➤ a Passover?

Jesus knew He would be sacrificed for us, and that He would pay the price of our rebellions, of our sins. True believers have been marked with the blood of the Lamb and therefore eternal judgment passes over us – and is laid to Jesus' account. These verses help to place this in context:

For by the blood of Christ we are set free, that is, our sins are forgiven. How great is the grace of God (Ephesians 1:7).

For you know what was paid to set you free from the worthless manner of life handed down by your ancestors. It was not something that can be destroyed, such as silver or gold; it was the costly sacrifice of Christ, who was like a lamb without defect or flaw (1 Peter 1:18-19).

God bought you for a price; so do not become slaves of people. (1 Corinthians 7:23)

But by the free gift of God's grace all are put right with him through Christ Jesus, who sets them free. God offered him, so that by his blood he should become the means by which people's sins are forgiven through their faith in him. God did this in order to demonstrate that he is righteous. In the past he was patient and overlooked people's sins; but in the present time he deals with their sins, in order to demonstrate his righteousness. In this way God shows that he himself is righteous and that he puts right everyone who believes in Jesus. (Romans 3:24-25)

... by whom we are set free, that is, our sins are forgiven. (Colossians 1:14)

So keep watch over yourselves and over all the flock which the Holy Spirit has placed in your care. Be shepherds of the church of God, which he made his own through the blood of his Son. (Acts 20:28)

What, then, of those who despise the Son of God? Who treat as a cheap thing the blood of God's covenant which purified them from sin? Who insult the Spirit of grace? Just think how much worse is the punishment they will deserve! (Hebrews 10:29).

God patiently, throughout the Tanakh (the Old Testament), pointed forwards towards His Messiah Who would come to save the world, and so God slowly and progressively revealed His plan of salvation. Hence in Genesis 3:14-15, right at the very beginning of the Bible, we see the announcement of the judgment of God upon the devil (the "serpent"). The spiritual battle between God and the devil – through the devil's proxy, the "offspring" of the woman – would be decisively resolved by a "he" who would "crush" Satan's head. Normative Christian theology affirms that the "he" is Jesus the Messiah. But how would this happen? And why was mankind banished from Eden?

To answer the second question first: if mankind was not expelled from Eden then God's rescue plan, centred on the Messiah, could not be effected. Accordingly, man would not, ultimately, be able to enter into "God's rest"[4] – that is, God's special and eternal provision for His chosen peoples. Mankind would then be condemned eternally to death with no possibility of redemption through Messiah. Forced by God to stand on his own two feet, we might say, mankind could painstakingly be prepared to encounter its Saviour, at a defined and definitive point in history (at Calvary).[5] To answer the first question (*How* would Jesus "crush" Satan's head?): we need to reflect that God's primary purpose was not to defeat the devil – the outcome of the eternal battle has never been in doubt – defeat and destruction of the devil was (is) inevitable. God's primary purpose was to "choose" a family He could call His Own and which would be with Him throughout eternity. So God progressively revealed His purpose and His plan. God would definitively defeat the devil by defeating the only ultimately effective weapon with which Satan can afflict us – death itself. Jesus' lordship over death is demonstrated, is proved, by the resurrection.

God chose a people – the Hebrews – through His covenant with Abraham. Abraham's family line would be "reckoned" (or counted) through Isaac. In Genesis chapter 22 Abraham's faith is tested, as God instructs Abraham to sacrifice his only son (22:2). It should be noted that Isaac was no mere boy at this time. We know for example that his brother Ishmael was grown up and married (21:21) and the age difference between them was at most a few years. It was "some time" after the treaty at Beersheba[6] that Abraham was tested by God, so some commentators suggest that Isaac was potentially in his early thirties at this time; irrespective, he was almost certainly at his physical prime and therefore no mere little boy, as so often depicted in the illustrations in children's Bibles! Isaac willingly placed himself in his father's hands (22:29). Isaac could successfully have resisted, but chose not to. In this we are reminded of Jesus Who went willingly to fulfil His Father's purposes (John 10:18). Isaac was spared. Jesus would not be spared. God Himself provided the sacrifice, just as Abraham had foretold (22:8); and what did God provide? A ram (a fully grown male sheep) caught by its head in a thicket (22:13). Its head was caught, if you like, in a crown of thorns (Matthew 27:29). We conclude that the sacrificial death "passed over" Isaac and was instead paid by the sacrificial ram.

The clearest "type" of the Passover of Jesus on behalf of mankind is revealed to us in the events surrounding the release of the children of Israel from bondage in Egypt. We move on to Exodus 12 to explore what is today universally understood to be *the* Passover event. In brief; in order to compel Pharaoh to release the Hebrew captives, God passes through Egypt and strikes down the first born (12:12). Only those whose dwellings are marked with the blood of a sacrificed year-old unblemished lamb are spared (12:12-13). This event is the basis of the Hebrew "feast" of Passover (Deuteronomy 16:1-8). The fact that this is a permanent ordinance for Jewish people explains why Jesus faithfully kept the Passover feast. He knew in any case, that He would be *the* Passover Lamb for all time.

Today liberal theologians and churchmen look with great disdain at what they like to call the "butcher shop" gospel. A well-known British liberal referred to the penal substitution of Christ as "cosmic child abuse", so providing the media and press with a neat soundbite to disparage the good news of Jesus' accomplishment on the cross. By contrast, Phillip Keller explores the theological and biological truth that life only emerges from death.[7] Keller describes these liberals as showing "great naivety" in failing to understand the combined scientific and spiritual principle at work in the universe.[8] We note that, by providing clear instructions in Exodus 12 to the Israelite slaves in Egypt, God established a pattern with deep spiritual significance. He instructed the Hebrews to consume the flesh of the sacrificed lamb in its entirety in one night. Not only would the blood daubed on their door lintels provide protection from the destroying angel (in a real sense, protection from 'judgment' by the angel) but also the lamb's meat would energise them for the arduous escape from Egypt and the eventual "passing over" the Red Sea to freedom.

It is astounding that historical truth (the flight of the Hebrew nation from Egypt) should so precisely mirror spiritual truth, that Jesus is the sacrificial lamb, slain from before the beginning of the world (1 Peter 1:20 and Revelation 13:8). Let us, as a short excursus, summarise this in a simple diagram:

An historical truth

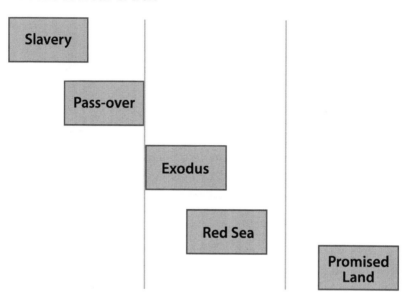

As we understand the chronology from the Bible, the events portrayed in Exodus involved slavery, the passing-over event (which we can see, in a very real sense involves both the Passover meal, the associated "salvation" from the destroying angel, as well as the later passing over the Red Sea and the associated "salvation" from the pursuing Egyptian chariot army) and eventual transition, forty years later, to the promised land. The captivity in Egypt was something from which the Hebrew people were powerless to deliver themselves. Constantly they needed God's "salvation" power to rescue them. We might say that, theologically, the events worked themselves out in a series of steps, as depicted here:

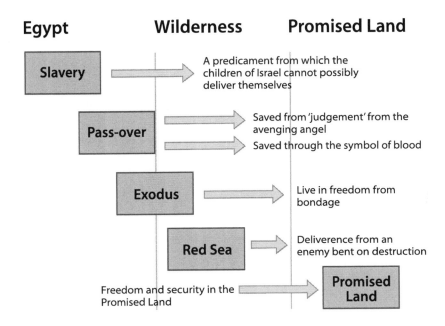

These historical truths mirror the spiritual truth that all mankind is locked-in to the reality of sin – rebellion against God, whether that rebellion is conscious or unconscious. Can we say that mankind suffers, spiritually, from "locked-in syndrome"? We humans just cannot wean ourselves off the tragedy of sin, we are locked-in with it. But God has graciously provided an escape route, as our next diagram illustrates:

Historical truth reflects spiritual truth ......

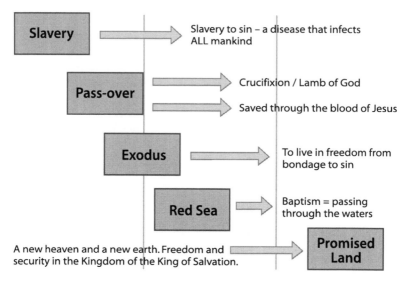

This chapter is not the place to fully explore and resolve the assertions encompassed in these diagrams, but it is hoped that they "map out", in a basic way, these profound truths. By the same token we cannot here explore the astonishing truths around the use of a "Scapegoat" as part of the Leviticus 16:20-22 ritual, as these more detailed sacrificial instructions also anticipate the atoning work of the Messiah. Nor can we here explore the amazing truths expressed in both Psalm 22 and Isaiah chapters 52 and 53, where we encounter the most graphic representation of the future crucifixion of Jesus, Son of God. These are wonderful themes indeed, but simply beyond the scope of a single chapter. They do, however, add depth and breadth to our understanding of God's salvific purposes and are well worth exploration in their own right.

We note that there are in fact seven Moedim established by God as the meetings (or "appointed times", "assemblies" or "holy convocations") for His people to come before Him and to recognise His great salvation plan. Each of the Moedim speak powerfully into the life, mission, ministry and achievement of Jesus – and of God's holy salvific purposes.

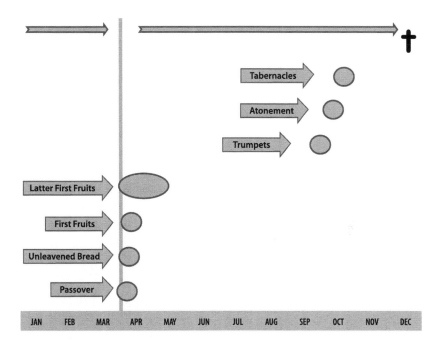

It is genuinely sad that the majority of church-attending Christians live in such profound ignorance of the seven Moedim and how they work together, but we do appear today to be witnessing a resurgence of understanding as well as a heartfelt rejoicing in this rediscovery.

The first Moed in any year (whether a solar or lunar year) is Passover. Jesus is our Passover Lamb. Through being the sacrificial Lamb of God, Jesus takes away the sins of the world (John 1:29). Jesus' last meal before His crucifixion was the Passover supper. Jesus is, in a very real sense, the second Moses Who *leads His people from the Egypt of sin and delivers them safely into the promised land of salvation*. Those who are disciples of Jesus from the Hebrew (Jewish) people are arguably God's "first fruits" (the third Moedim). Those who follow Jesus from amongst the non-Jews ("Gentiles") are the *Latter First Fruits* (the fourth Moed – although this ordering in no way implies any hierarchy in God's favours, for all alike have sinned and fall short of the glory of God; all alike must be saved by and through Jesus the Messiah. There are no second-class citizens in the Kingdom of God. God was always going to enlarge His chosen people to have representatives from every tribe and tongue. God's Kingdom is expansive and expanded, consisting of *all* those who place their faith and trust in the Messiah, truly repenting of sins. The offer of life and eternal security in the Kingdom *is open to all*; there are no exceptions, and no excuses either. All those who trust[9] in Jesus will be saved eternally. Those who are lost eternally are lost because they reject Jesus.

The Lord Jesus will return to take His rightful place as King of His Kingdom, reigning eternally on David's throne. The time when the Lord returns will be, we can be 99.9% certain, at the Feast of Trumpets (the fifth Moed). We will explore this elsewhere and provide the necessary evidences. If we want to be promoted to Jesus' Kingdom of disciples, to be given a brand new life lived in Him, then we must be passed over for that promotion! That is really what is entailed in, and meant by, the theological term *the penal substitution of Messiah*. God must "see" us marked with the blood of the sacrificial lamb, marked with the blood of *the* Lamb. It is through the blood that eternal peace is purchased. This is a bill we simply cannot pay ourselves. The "cost" of our sins is finally laid to Jesus' account. The bill is, as they say, paid on the nail.

These are wonderful truths indeed. No wonder God made Passover a permanent ordinance for His chosen people, who (praise God) continue to mark and observe the Passover feast right down to our own day. How sad that even today so many Jewish people fail to see the ultimate fulfillment of Passover in Messiah Yeshua, the Passover Lamb. Yet how sad also that so many professed Christians similarly fail truly to perceive the eternal significance of Passover and instead mark a pagan festival called "Easter"[10] (which "feast" incidentally, God nowhere commanded nor authorised). As for myself, as the author of this book, I am happy to be *passed over – for promotion* and to rejoice in the glorious certainty that because Messiah Jesus gave His life in exchange for mine, so I can spend eternity in the presence of my Saviour, the Prince of Peace.

Notes

[1] Physical Education lesson.

[2] It is interesting that the Exodus account in the Bible does not mention the name of the Pharaoh. Since Moses was the author, he certainly *could have* named Pharaoh. So why didn't he? I believe that Pharaoh's name is intentionally omitted. Throughout the Exodus narrative, Pharaoh either implies or asks "*Who is the Lord that I should obey his voice to let Israel go? I do not know the Lord, nor will I let Israel go*" (Ex. 5:2). The irony, surely intentional, is that we don't know Pharaoh's name, but we do know the Lord's name (Yahweh – "I AM"). The book of Exodus was not written to exalt the Egyptian Pharaoh (who was considered to be a "divine god-king"), but rather the God of Israel.

[3] Of course there are many spiritual lessons around Passover that re-emphasise this. I draw readers' attention to Philip Keller's lovely short book *A Shepherd Looks at the Lamb of God* (ISBN 0720805279) which appears still to be widely available in 2016.

[4] This concept is fully developed in Hebrews chapters 3 and 4.

[5] Golgotha – the place of the skull

[6] Genesis 21:22-34

[7] *A Shepherd Looks at The Lamb of God*, Phillip Keller, Bethany House, 1982.

[8] Op Cit page 46

[9] This trusting is normally evidenced in repentance, baptism and new life. See David Pawson, *The Normal Christian Birth: How to Give New Believers a Proper Start in Life*, published 1997 but still widely available.

[10] Your author intends to be challenging in this statement. Christians seek, with some genuine heartfelt impetus, to mark a clear memorial of the Resurrection, yet have adopted or co-opted the pagan fertility celebration of Easter. To call this "unfortunate" is perhaps an understatement. Passover marks the crucifixion yet Biblically it is First Fruits that marks the resurrection, as we shall see in Chapter 7.

PART 2

THE MOEDIM – THE JESUS PATTERN

Chapter 5

PASSOVER (CRUCIFIED)

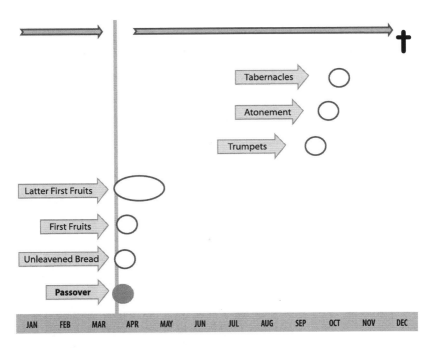

The First Passover

Then Moses summoned all the elders of Israel and said to them, "Go at once and select the animals for your families and slaughter the Passover lamb. Take a bunch of hyssop, dip it into the blood in the basin and put some of the blood on the top and on both sides of the door frame. None of you shall go out of the door of your house until morning. When the LORD goes through the land to strike down the Egyptians, he will see the blood on the top and sides of the door frame and will pass over that doorway, and he will not permit the destroyer to enter your houses and strike you down. "Obey these instructions as a lasting ordinance for you and your descendants.

When you enter the land that the LORD will give you as he promised, observe this ceremony. And when your children ask you, 'What does this ceremony mean to you?' then tell them, 'It is the Passover sacrifice to the LORD, who passed over the houses of the Israelites in Egypt and spared our homes when he struck down the Egyptians.' " Then the people bowed down and worshipped.

The Israelites did just what the LORD commanded Moses and Aaron.

(Exodus 12:21-28)

Passover – the Moed
These are the LORD's appointed festivals, the sacred assemblies you are to proclaim at their appointed times: The LORD's Passover begins at twilight on the fourteenth day of the first month.

(Leviticus 23:4-5)

Meaning
This Moed relates primarily to the miracle of the "exodus" from Egypt. The original Passover event recorded in Exodus chapter 12 involved a sacrifice. A year-old male lamb without defect (Ex 12:5) was selected; the method of spreading blood with hyssop (Ex 12:22) was detailed, as was disposal of the remains after the meal (Ex 12:10). All these testify to the sacrificial nature and meaning of the Passover.

The head of the family slays the lamb. The blood is a "sign" that the angel of death will spare those "covered" by the sacrifice. The whole point of the Passover is that the sacrifice of the lamb leads directly to the "salvation" of those who trust in (i.e. put their faith in) the efficacy of the blood of that lamb. By New Testament times the festivals of Passover and Unleavened Bread were well attended celebrations and were known as "the days of unleavened bread" (Luke 22:1; Acts 12:3). In Israelite life the early Passover and Unleavened Bread observances were comparatively simple in character, but during the Monarchy more elaborate Passover rituals came into use (2 Kings 23:21-23; 2 Chronicles 35:1-19).

Prophetic Fulfilment

Jesus is the Passover Lamb [Exodus 12:3; John 1:29; Romans 8:3] whose blood was shed from the beginning of the world [Revelation 13:8]. The crucifixion is prophesied clearly in Psalm 22 and Isaiah 52 – 53. The substitutionary sacrifice is set out in Genesis 22:1-14 (especially verse 8). This is the account of Abraham and his son Isaac, where we note that God had already promised to provide a substitute for sacrifice.

For observant Jews, the Passover speaks of the miracle of "salvation" *from* Pharaoh and *to* "freedom" in the Promised Land. But this is only a type of the real transaction. The ultimate and eternal fulfilment is found in the Messiah given for all mankind. Messiah atones for the sins of those who trust in the efficacy of the blood of *the* Lamb. Judgement passes over the penitent sinner and is placed to the account of the Messiah. Messiah is the sacrificial lamb.

Present Jewish Observance

The Passover was instituted by God [Leviticus 23:5; Exodus 12] and became a *permanent* Passover [Deuteronomy 16:1-8]. The Passover to the Rabbinic Jew today represents the "salvation" of the Hebrew people from their Egyptian owners. By contrast, the Passover to the Messianic Jew/Christian represents the salvation of those who place their faith in Jesus and their release from the slavery of sin.

Modern Jewish observance of Passover includes the consuming of lamb's flesh (Exodus 12:8). Bitter herbs and unleavened bread make up the simple meal, which is today called the Seder meal. We should note that today other, non-biblical, elements have been added to the traditional Jewish Seder meal – but the only elements actually commanded *as a lasting ordinance* are set out clearly in Exodus 12:1-8.

Re: Jesus

The Passover is a prototype of Yeshua's sacrifice. He is the perfect (sinless) Lamb who takes away the sins of the world. [1 John 1:7; 1 John 1:29; 1 Corinthians 5:7; 1 Peter 1:18-20]

Yeshua ate the Passover meal before He suffered crucifixion – Luke 22:13-15. Yeshua was well aware that He was the substitute "Lamb" Who would take away sins – theologians call this the "penal substitution" of Yeshua. He stands as the substitute *for* the penitent sinner, who no longer has to face punishment.

Commentary

For observant (religious/Rabbinic) Jews the Passover remains a foundational element of life and worship, yet its full prophetic meaning is lost to them. Pesach (Passover in Hebrew) is to these Jewish people purely the celebration of the historic deliverance of Israel from slavery in Egypt. Pesach to them marks in a very real sense the birth of their nation and both the calling and the freedom to worship the one true God. Throughout history, Pesach is celebrated on 14 Nisan, the first month of the Jewish religious calendar. Jesus was crucified and died on the day of Passover. He was buried before sunset and lay in the tomb on the first three nights of the feast of Unleavened Bread. He was resurrected physically from death on the day of First Fruits.

Reverting to the very first Passover, we recall that the children of Israel were terribly mistreated during their captivity in Egypt, initially because Pharaoh was afraid that they were becoming too numerous (Ex 1:8-14). God was fully aware of this unjust abuse and had "decided" on a plan of rescue (Ex 3:16-17), which involved Moses delivering the simple message to Pharaoh to "let My people go" (5:1).[1] Nine times Pharaoh refused God's demand, and nine times plagues of various types were visited upon the land of Egypt. Finally, God told Moses that He would send "one more" plague, and that after this, Pharaoh would comply. Following this terrible final "plague", involving the death of the first-born, the Israelites were allowed to leave – and so began their extended journey towards their promised land.[2]

Up until this time there had been only one (civil) calendar which the Jews followed. It began in the month of Tishri (equivalent to our September-October). It was in the seventh month of this civil calendar that God told Moses about the tenth and final "plague" on Egypt, in the month of Nisan (our March). In Exodus 12:2 God told Moses that this month, Nisan, would be the first month of the cycle in a new *religious calendar* on which the timing of all of future religious festivals would be based.

The details of the Passover Moed were to be as follows: on Nisan 10 each household would select a lamb without defect. Each such lamb was to be cared for by the family until Nisan 14, when it was sacrificed at twilight. At the original Passover, its blood was daubed on the door lintel and side posts – and some commentators suggest that this may be symbolic of the cross of crucifixion, in its vertical and horizontal axes. Sacrificing the Passover lamb would become a ceremony to be observed as a lasting ordinance (Ex 12:24; Lev 23:5) *for all generations*. It was on Nisan 10 that Jesus made His final entrance into Jerusalem. Just prior to His descent from the Mount of Olives into the city of Jerusalem, the annual procession of the national Passover lamb was taking place. This lamb, which would carry the sins of the nation, was taken to the Temple ready for sacrifice on Nisan 14. It was led into the city from the east and would be met by crowds of people waving palm branches and joyfully singing Psalm 118 as they celebrated the miraculous delivery of their ancestors from Egyptian slavery. The lamb was open for scrutiny for four days so that everyone and anyone[3] could see it was free from defect – that it was perfect.

Following the procession of the Passover lamb, Jesus descended from the Mount of Olives, riding on a donkey. He would have followed precisely the same path to the Temple that the earlier lamb had travelled. During the following four days, whilst the sacrificial lamb was on view for inspection by the people, Jesus was in a very real sense being scrutinised by the religious authorities in Jerusalem – they interrogated Him, yet He always left them speechless. They could find no fault with Him (Matthew 21:23-27; 22: 23-46; 26:59-60; Luke 23:4, 14-15; John 19:6). This was because Jesus, also, was *perfect* and *without defect*, just as the sacrificial lamb had to be.

The national Passover lamb would be sacrificed in the Temple on Nisan 14 at twilight (Ex 12:6), having been bound to the altar at about 09.00 AM and finally sacrificed at 3.00 PM. It is notable that Jesus was in the process of crucifixion (if we can reverently call it that) during the same hours. He hung on the cross until He died at 3.00 PM ("the ninth hour"). As the High Priest killed the lamb, he would have announced "it is finished", meaning that the Chosen People were once again free from their sins. On the cross at Glogotha, just a few miles away, Jesus' last words recorded by John were also "it is finished" (John 19:30). In the same way, His chosen people (from every tribe and tongue) were now free from the bondage of their sins.

We can speculate quite reasonably that the Lord Jesus knew intimately the details of the Temple ritual, and that in a very real sense Jesus timed His death to coincide with the slaughter of the Temple lamb. Jesus had already stated plainly: "No one takes [my life] from me, but I lay it don of my own accord. I have authority to lay it down and to take it up again" (John 10:18). Moments before He died, Jesus called out, "Father, into your hands I commit my spirit" (Matthew 27:50). He knew that He had to keep the appointment of dying at the same time as the Passover lamb in the Temple, as well as to leave sufficient time to be buried before the feast of Unleavened Bread began at sunset.

We can summarise, then, by stating that the Passover is a "type" of the crucifixion. The counterpoints between the ceremony of Passover and the reality of crucifixion (of shadow versus substance) are too numerous for mere coincidence, especially when taken in context of the other six Moedim that speak so eloquently of Jesus' mission and ministry.

Notes
[1] The One New Man Bible expresses this more forcefully. "Let My people go" might sound like a request. In fact it was a command. The One New Man Bible renders this as "send My people away", which is probably a closer rendering of the original.
[2] To some people it may sound "cruel" that God would visit such a plague on the "innocents" of Egypt. This is perhaps an unduly sentimentalised view of "innocence" versus "guilt" as we remember that the entire Egyptian Empire and social order was built upon the economic foundations of slavery – who then was truly innocent of that evil? This, however, is surely not the point. It *was* painful to God to visit this terrible event upon the Egyptians, but was it not just as terrible that God's first-born (indeed only) Son had the penalty of sin visited upon Him – that He would be cut off on account of other people's sins? We need to remember that the sins for which He died were not His Own, for He was sinless – He died on account of your sins and my sins! Why should the innocent Jesus die for you and me? Where is the "justice" in that ?
[3] If they were Jewish.

Chapter 6

UNLEAVENED BREAD (BURIED)

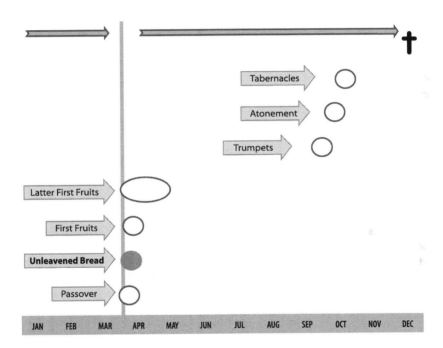

On the fifteenth day of that month the LORD's Festival of Unleavened Bread begins; for seven days you must eat bread made without yeast. On the first day hold a sacred assembly and do no regular work. For seven days present a food offering to the LORD. And on the seventh day hold a sacred assembly and do no regular work.

(Leviticus 23:6-8)

Meaning

On the evening after Passover and for seven days thereafter, God commanded the Hebrew people to consume bread made without yeast [Leviticus 23:1, 4-6]. This was instituted as the permanent Passover meal, reflective of the original Passover meal, where again unleavened bread was to be consumed (Exodus 12:8). [See also Deuteronomy 16:3]. We need to note carefully that the bread has no yeast – remembering that yeast is, biblically, a symbol of sin. The bread consumed during the Moed of Unleavened Bread is a poignant reminder of the need to live without sin.

The command to remove yeast from the bread mix was not simply because of the need to cook and eat the meal quickly, as some commentators have suggested. The original command (Exodus 12:8) urged the Hebrews to understand the depth of their plight and their need to be freed from slavery. The meaning today is equally urgent: for everyone on planet Earth it is the need to flee from sin [2 Timothy 2:19] and to live on the holy bread that sustains [John 6:48-49]. This means that we recognise our need of God's forgiveness through Jesus, turning to Him in faith and repentance, and we "feed" upon Him for the remainder of our lives.

Prophetic Fulfilment

Leaven (yeast) is a symbol of death and decay.[1] The rise in dough is only possible by a natural process of decay. Yeshua is without sin and accordingly His body saw no decay, in spite of the fact that it was dead and buried [Acts 2:14-37 and Acts 13:37]. Partaking of *this* bread (Yeshua) means that we humbly identify with the sufferings and afflictions that Jesus encountered on our behalf [Isaiah 53:4-5]. The Hebrew word variously translated as "blow" or "wound" or "stripe" (Isaiah 53:5) comes from the same root as "friend" – it could be read as "by His friendship we are healed". See John 15:13 and Proverbs 18:24.

Present Jewish Observance

Today the feast of Unleavened Bread is subsumed by observant Jews into their annual festival of "Passover" – however the Passover is in reality a 24-hour period whereas the Feast of Unleavened Bread lasts for seven days. We can say that, sadly, this Moed is effectively "lost" to most Jewish people, and yet it was commanded by their G-d.

Today's "Matzo",[2] which is supposed to be eaten during these seven days, has stripes that look like the bruises inflicted by beating, and the Matzo is pierced through with holes. The Rabbinic tradition is to cook quickly (18 minutes) and hence cooking on a griddle with the associated piercings. The Rabbinic tradition, however, unwittingly reflects the reality that Jesus was pierced and bruised for us [Isaiah 53:5-6].

Today's commemoration amongst observant Rabbinic Jews reflects the reality of salvation from slavery, but it ignores the reality of the spiritual need for salvation from slavery to sin. The bread that is supposed to sustain them is without yeast – that is, without sin.

Re: Jesus

Yeshua is the Passover Lamb [John 1:29; John 3:36; Acts 8:32-36; 1 Corinthians 5:7-8; 1 Peter 1:18-20] . Scripture reveals that the offering of the first-fruits is a picture of the resurrection [1 Corinthians 15:20-23; Romans 8:23; James 1:18]. Although dead and buried, because He is sinless His body can see no decay [Acts 2:22; Acts13:37; Psalm 16:10]. Yeshua (Jesus) was sacrificed for us. Having been killed, He was buried, but quite literally the grave could not hold Him. When we become believers, we are "buried" with Him [Romans 6:4; Colossians 2:12] and having been buried with Him, so we shall rise as He did.

Like the grain of wheat, Jesus was buried, and like the "dead" grain, He rises with a great harvest. [John 12:24]. We reflect also on the awesome statement that Jesus made in John 6:48: **"I am the bread of life"**. Let us read this in context. Jesus had recently undertaken the amazing miracle of feeding 5,000 people. His "fame" had spread abroad and accordingly people were actively seeking Him out. Many of them could have been asking, inwardly if not outwardly: is this the promised Messiah?

"Very truly I tell you, you are looking for me, not because you saw the signs I performed but because you ate the loaves and had your fill. Do not work for food that spoils, but for food that endures to eternal life, which the Son of Man will give you. For on him God the Father has placed his seal of approval."

Then they asked him, "What must we do to do the works God requires?"

Jesus answered, "The work of God is this: to believe in the one he has sent."

So they asked him, "What sign then will you give that we may see it and believe you? What will you do? Our ancestors ate the manna in the wilderness; as it is written: 'He gave them bread from heaven to eat.' "

Jesus said to them, "Very truly I tell you, it is not Moses who has given you the bread from heaven, but it is my Father who gives you the true bread from heaven. For the bread of God is the bread that comes down from heaven and gives life to the world."

"Sir," they said, "always give us this bread."

Then Jesus declared, "I am the bread of life. Whoever comes to me will never go hungry, and whoever believes in me will never be thirsty".

(John 6:26-35).

Commentary

Leaven (or yeast) is a substance added to dough to make it ferment and rise. Only a small quantity is required for this purpose. The use of leaven in the making of bread was well known to ancient people. Leavening took time and was of no use when there was need to make a hurried meal. From the earliest times the Hebrews attached spiritual meaning to leaven and associated the leavening process with creeping corruption. Even the smallest quantity was forbidden to be found in Jewish houses at the time of the Feast of Unleavened Bread. This exclusion of leaven represented, spiritually, the requirement of the Redeemed to live holy lives in communion with God and the Covenant community. We should note carefully that leaven could not be in any offering which pointed forwards to the propitiatory sacrifice of Messiah, the sinless Lamb of God. This is a point lost upon Rabbinic Judaism. Indeed, in the Bible leaven speaks consistently of evil, as these passages demonstrate:

Gen.19:1-3 (cf.18:6); Ex.12:8,11; Jdg.6:19-22
Ex.12:14-15,34-39, 13:3,6-7, 23:18; Lev.23:6-8; Dt.16:3-8
Lev.2:11, 6:17, 10:12
Num.6:13-20
Hos.7:4

In the New Testament, leaven is associated, symbolically, with false teaching and hypocrisy – an outward faith that has no corresponding inner reality. Just as leaven works in a hidden way to permeate the dough and increase its mass, so corruption can be an unheeded process which gradually spreads and bloats. Thus, the Parable of the Leaven (Mt **13**:3; Luke **13**: 20-21) is arguably no exception to the usual Biblical symbolism. Certainly, the parable gives no indication that leaven is here being used differently – and therefore surprisingly – to represent a good influence (which is sometimes argued). Jesus is warning that false teaching and influences will infiltrate and adulterate the Church which will become bloated in its extent by merely external religion and those who do not truly belong to Christ. Christians should be wary of the spread of corrupting elements and seek to live holy lives as the true Redeemed of the Lord:

Mt.16:6,11-12; Mk.8:15; Lk.12:1-3
1 Cor.5:6-13; Gal.5:7-9; (cf. also 2 Cor.7:1; 2 Tim.4:3-4; 2 Pet.2:1-2)
Lk.13:20-21

For observant (religious / Rabbinic) Jews today the Passover remains a key element of their national life. Yet it is "performed" (and I think that is not an unfair verb) in a manner at variance with the simple and straightforward requirements of the Tanakh. And this Rabbinic "Passover" has absorbed and eliminated the biblically separate Moed of Unleavened Bread. Whether this is to avoid the challenging implication of the burial of their Messiah is a moot point: what is beyond (reasonable) dispute is that the burial of the *suffering servant* was prefigured by the prophet Isaiah: **"He was assigned a grave with the wicked, and with the rich in his death, though he had done no violence, nor was any deceit in his mouth"**. (Isaiah 53:9). It was prefigured also by the

Psalmist David: **"My body will also rest secure, because you will not abandon me to the grave, nor will you let your Holy One see decay"**. (Psalm 16:9-10).

We can say with assurance, therefore, that the Moed of Passover speaks of the "salvation" of God's *chosen people* (no matter what their ethnicity) through the sacrifice of the suffering servant of Isaiah 53. The Moed of Unleavened Bread affirms that this sinless Saviour would indeed lie in the grave – in fact He would lie in a rich man's grave[3] – and yet His body would "see" no "corruption"; bluntly, that it would not putrefy. Instead it would be raised, as our next study affirms. Only a sinless Saviour could be raised in this way, and the unleavened bread is symbolic of His sinlessness, being without leaven.

The last point we should note is that Jesus stated emphatically: *I am the bread of life* (see John 6:48). As He uttered these words in the synagogue at Capernaum He was no doubt anticipating His ultimate sacrifice on behalf of mankind (and on behalf of you and me personally!). He knew already that He is the unleavened bread that would lie for three days in the grave but *without corruption*. Jesus' statement that He is the bread of life was thoroughly astounding! He made it in the context of the aftermath of the feeding of the five thousand, following which we are told that the crowds actively "sought" Him (John 6:24). Jesus assessed their interest in Him bluntly: **"you are looking for me because you ate the bread and had all you wanted, not because you understood my miracles. Do not work for food that goes bad; instead work for the food that lasts for eternal life."** Jesus was gently refocusing their attention away from their stomachs and towards Him. Indeed, in the phrase "work for" Jesus was certainly reminding those who seek to follow Him that there will be an element of "work" involved. As we choose to follow Him we do enter into a lifetime of joyful service.

The crowds who followed Jesus at this point still failed to grasp His wonderful message; they asked for a "sign" (6:30-31) as though they had not already had one (6:1-15)! In His reply Jesus again pointed towards the unleavened bread **"what Moses gave you was not *the* bread from heaven; it is my Father who gives you the *real* bread from heaven. For the bread that God gives is He Who comes down from heaven and gives life to the world"**.[4] (Author's emphasis.) It was a wonderful truth, but it was only dimly perceived by those to whom Jesus was speaking. Their response? **"Sir ... give us this bread always"** (6:34). It is at this point, in verse 35 that Jesus makes the astounding statement that it is He Who is the bread of life – and in this we can say that not only is He the bread who sustains in this life, He is also the bread that sustains throughout eternity. Jesus' message caused "grumbling" amongst the Jews, and it still does to this day! But it is not only Jews that "grumble" about this, we can say that those of the world's religions will often "grumble" about Jesus' assertion – as do those of no religion whatsoever! We have only to think of the considerable number of "atheists" who hate the message of Jesus. The Lord's teaching was too strong for many, but these people were still not making the connection between their Feast of Unleavened Bread and the truths that Jesus was preaching. Jesus went on:

"I am telling you the truth: he who believes has eternal life.

I am the bread of life. Your ancestors ate manna in the desert, but they died. But the bread that comes down from heaven is of such a kind that whoever eats it will not die. I am the living bread that came down from heaven. If you eat this bread, you will live forever. The bread that I will give you is my flesh, which I give so that the world may live." This started an angry argument among them. "How can this man give us his flesh to eat?" they asked. Jesus said to them, "I am telling you the truth: if you do not eat the flesh of the Son of Man and drink his blood, you will not have life in yourselves. Those who eat my flesh and drink my blood have eternal life, and I will raise them to life on the last day. For my flesh is the real food; my blood is the real drink. Those who eat my flesh and drink my blood live in me, and I live in them. The living Father sent me, and because of Him I live also. In the same way whoever eats me will live because of me. This, then, is the bread that came down from heaven; it is not like the bread that your ancestors ate, but then later died. Those who eat this bread will live forever." (John 6:47-58, GNT).

Those who eat this bread will live forever! We can straightforwardly make the connection between the unleavened "bread" consumed at

Passover, which was a precursor to freedom, and the unleavened bread of the "feast" of the following seven days, and the bread that Jesus told His disciples to eat "in remembrance of me" at the last supper. The Church's "communion" elements of bread and wine of course speak of the body and blood of the Saviour, shed for all mankind, but in their modern form they rather lose the wonderful truths of Unleavened Bread, a period of reflection following Passover, when we should daily think upon the awesome truth of a buried Saviour Who sees no corruption, and so guarantees that His followers, also, will see no corruption.

Notes
[1] Diligent readers who want to dig into this can freely access online "The Bible Student" and study number 40 (Leaven/Yeast)
[2] Matzo, plural matzot, is an unleavened flatbread that is part of modern Jewish cuisine. It forms an integral element of the modern Jewish Passover festival. Matzo that is kosher for Passover is limited in the Ashkenazi tradition to plain matzo made from flour and water.
[3] Each of the four Gospels confirms that Joseph of Arimathea applied to Pilate to take Jesus' dead body and to lay it in his own private grave plot: Matthew 27:57 is specific that Joseph of Arimathea was "rich".
[4] Emphases added by the author.

Chapter 7

FIRST FRUITS (RESURRECTION)

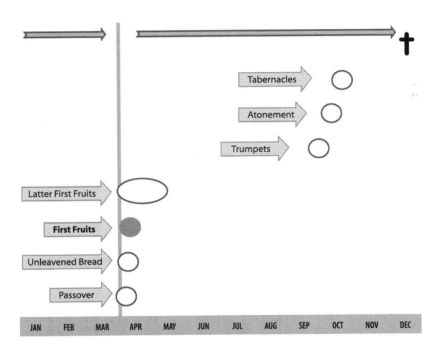

The LORD said to Moses, "Speak to the Israelites and say to them: 'When you enter the land I am going to give you and you reap its harvest, bring to the priest a sheaf of the first grain you harvest. He is to wave the sheaf before the LORD so it will be accepted on your behalf; the priest is to wave it on the day after the Sabbath. On the day you wave the sheaf, you must sacrifice as a burnt offering to the LORD a lamb a year old without defect, together with its grain

offering of two-tenths of an ephah of the finest flour mixed with olive oil—a food offering presented to the LORD, a pleasing aroma—and its drink offering of a quarter of a hin of wine. You must not eat any bread, or roasted or new grain, until the very day you bring this offering to your God. This is to be a lasting ordinance for the generations to come, wherever you live.

(Leviticus 23:9-14)

Meaning

An acknowledgement of God's bounty and providence to Israel. By consecration of the first-fruits of the harvest (the so-called "Harvest Festival" of the *institutional church* is an interesting, if erroneous, parallel) the Israelites proclaim that not only the first fruits, but also the entire harvest, belongs to God (see Leviticus 23:10-11 and 12-14).

The sacrifice of a year-old unblemished lamb simply echoes the Passover sacrifice. The offering of grain and wine at the conclusion of this "third feast of Passover" is emblematic of the body and blood of Jesus – His body "given" for all mankind. Not only believing Jews belong to God's Kingdom (as first fruits), but believers from every tribe and tongue, from every ethnic group, belong to God's Kingdom (the entire harvest). That is truly good news! But note that there is an order in God's plan – First Fruits is *followed* by the full harvest.

The meaning of this Holy Day can be better understood from its Hebrew name – Sfirat HaOmer – literally "the counting of the sheaves". It refers to the earliest harvest that took place in Israel, the barley harvest. As Leviticus tells us, the first cut sheaves of the barley were to be brought to the priest as an offering in the Tabernacle (or later the Temple). Its lesson was clear: as God had been faithful to bless the land with this early harvest, so He would most certainly provide the full harvest of the later summer. In the days of the Temple the First Fruits ceremony was an elaborate undertaking. The Talmud states that a priest would meet with each group of Jewish pilgrims on the edge of the city and from there lead them up to the Temple Mount. As they carried their offering toward the Temple, the priest would lead a praise service with dance, music and psalms of praise. Once arrived at the Temple, the priest would take the sheaves, lift some of them into the air and wave them in each direction. In so doing, the whole assembly would be acknowledging God's provision and sovereignty over the entire earth. By this consecration of the first fruits, the people of Israel were proclaiming publicly that they offered not just the first fruits, but also the entire harvest to God – *because* it had been provided by Him.

Prophetic Fulfilment

The first fruit is offered to God to acknowledge His bounty and goodness in providing the harvest – all of which belongs to Him. The first fruits is emblematic of the earliest saved and sanctified disciples of Yeshua. Yeshua Himself is the first to be raised to new life in a new, resurrected, body. The earliest believers (we might say, the Jewish church was the proto-church) represent the first part of Jesus' global harvest, starting in the first century and extending throughout the "church age" (as some have called it). The whole of this harvest of believing souls belongs to God and is safely gathered in to His Kingdom.

Present Jewish Observance

This Moed seems largely to have been forgotten by Rabbinic Judaism. As with *Unleavened Bread*, it is effectively subsumed into Passover – the three have become blurred as one.

Leviticus 23:9-16
1 Corinthians 15:23
1 Thessalonians 4:13-18

The "waving of the omer" (or, in English, the waving of the sheaf, see Leviticus 23:11) has been entirely forgotten because, of course, there is today no Jerusalem Temple in which to undertake this biblical mandate. The waving of the omer has morphed into the so-called "counting of the omer" which (a) is nowhere commanded in Scripture and (b) is oddly associated with Latter First Fruits (Shavuout). See chapter 8.

Re: Jesus

"Messiah has indeed been raised from the dead, the first fruits of those who have fallen asleep. For since death came through a man,

**the resurrection of the dead comes also through a man. For as in
Adam all die, so in Messiah all will be made alive. But each in turn:
Messiah, the first fruits; then, when he comes, those who belong to
him"** (1 Corinthians 15:20-23).

Yeshua (in English, Jesus) is risen from the dead. The Bible is
emphatic about this and, as we saw above, this resurrection is both
fulfilled in prophecy and fulfilled in type – the most powerful "type"
being the seven Moedim and this First Fruits assembly.

He is the first-fruit of that far greater harvest – of all those who trust
in the efficacy of the blood of the Lamb. Jesus is the beginning of the
eternal harvest *for all time*. Jesus' resurrection, this prototype "early
harvest", marks the commencement of the New Covenant era, when *all*
who place their trust in the efficacy of the Lamb's blood are adopted into
His family. The Abraham covenant, enlarged by the Moses and Messiah
covenants, has effectively become the New Covenant (see Jeremiah
31:31); but in case anyone, especially Gentiles, get big-headed about
this, we must note clearly with *whom* this new covenant is "made". Note
also the future (eschatological?) dimension of this New Covenant, as
we began to explore in chapter 2. Some people are inclined to suggest
(problematically) that First Fruits ushers-in the "Church Age". Whilst
there is some validity in this idea, it fails to engage fully with the
prophetic significance of First Fruits.

Commentary
**But Christ has indeed been raised from the dead, the first-fruits of
those who have fallen asleep. For since death came through a man,
the resurrection of the dead comes also through a man. For as in
Adam all die, so in Christ all will be made alive. But each in turn:
Christ, the first-fruits; then, when he comes, those who belong to
him.** (1 Corinthians 15:20-23, NIV)

Believers today rejoice in the *fact* of our Lord's resurrection. We
could say that we are genuinely First Fruits People! Jesus is risen from
the dead, and as Paul expressed it to the Corinthian believers (above),
Christ is the first fruits of those who have died. We have to note that
there is a huge difference between the teachings of the various religions

– about some vague *immortality of the soul* – and the dependable truth of the resurrection of the body. Paganism accepts the immortality of the soul, but this is not the hope of the Believer. As Daniel Fuchs states in his helpful study *Israel's Holy Days in Type and Prophecy*:[1] "Our hope is not in an immortal, disembodied soul; it is in the resurrection of the body". Fuchs goes on: "Our Lord really died. His body was buried. He rose from the dead. The body of our Lord, which was resurrected, was the same body that died for us. Since He is the first fruits of the harvest, so also is the harvest *each in turn: Christ, the first-fruits; then, when he comes, those who belong to him* (1 Cor 15:23). This truth, says Fuchs, gives us abundant comfort. His study goes on with two useful pages about the resurrection body as explored in Scripture.[2]

There are two ways of looking at this Holy Day, or Moed, of First Fruits. It is abundantly clear that the *risen* Messiah is the first fruits of God's redeeming grace. That is what the first three Moedim collectively are leading towards – crucifixion, burial and resurrection. It's all about Jesus! There is a sub-text to this however. The first fruits of God's ultimate harvest may also be seen as the Jewish believers in Jesus down through history. The apostle Paul certainly regarded the earliest Hebrew believers in Messiah in precisely this way, as the first fruits of the Israel of God (Romans 11:16). We recall that the first century proto-church was almost entirely Jewish. The apostle Paul affirmed that the gospel was to be taken to the Jew first and *then* to the Gentile (Romans 1:16). So to see the *first fruits* as Jewish believers in Christ, and the *latter first fruits* as the Gentile believers is a reasonable extension of the idea. In this case those first fruits would be Jewish believers in aggregate down through the history of the post-ascension church. Another way of viewing the first fruits would be to consider them as being the entire apostolic proto-church whether Jew or Gentile, as differentiated from those of the post-apostolic period through to our own day. Since our scriptures explore the wonderful truth of Jewish and non-Jewish believers equally receiving the good news of Jesus, this also is a helpful understanding of what First Fruits is all about.

There is, in Messiah Jesus, no difference between Jew and Gentile. (Romans 10:12-13; Galatians 3:28; Colossians 3:11). Indeed one of the amazing triumphs of the gospel is the creation of "one new man" out of the two, of Jew and Gentile (Ephesians 2:15) united in Messiah. This is the motif of the *One New Man Bible*[3] ("ONMB") which is a useful modern translation that seeks to highlight both the Godly power and authority given to believers, as well as the Hebraic idiom of so much of our Scriptures. As the ONMB usefully renders it:

"For He is our peace, the One Who has made both things into one and Who has loosed the dividing wall of the fence, cause of the enmity to His flesh, by His nullifying the tradition of the commandments by decrees, so that He could create the two, Jewish and non-Jewish, into One New Man, establishing peace so he could reconcile both in one body to God through the cross, as God killed their enmity by means of Y'shua. And when He came He proclaimed the good news of peace to you, to those far away, and peace to those near; because through Him we both have the introduction to the Father by means of one Spirit. Therefore then, you are no longer aliens and strangers, but are fellow citizens of the saints and members of the household of God, building upon the foundation of the apostles and prophets, Messiah Y'shua being His cornerstone, in whom the whole building is being fit together into a habitation of God by the Spirit".

(Ephesians 2:14-22, ONMB)

Wow! This is pretty amazing stuff! Read it several times to get its full impact. There is a division within mankind which the Bible renders as Jew and Gentile, or more correctly (and less palatably) Jew and heathen. Too often this distinction boils down to Jew *versus* Gentile and Gentile *versus* Jew. One has only to think of the persecutions against Jews down through three millennia even to our own day – and this, sometimes, emanating from within the institutional church. But God had a plan expressed from the beginning of time, to have *one* united family, in which there are no spiritual differences. There may be cultural differences. There may in God's eschatological plan be missional differences and differences in focus and emphasis. We have only to remember the Apostle Paul's statement that the Messiah's body (the church) is a body with many distinct parts. These parts are not in competition with each other, but they each have distinct tasks to carry out in the life of the whole. (See 1 Corinthians 12:12-31).

In the portion from Ephesians chapter 2 above, the "two things" are Jew and non-Jew. The "dividing wall" is the abiding and often mutual mistrust between Jew and non-Jew. Those "far away" are "Gentiles". Those "near" are Jews – but both Jew and non-Jew are each in the *same* need of the saving power of Messiah Jesus. The "aliens and strangers" would normally be non-Jews, but in reality it is *anyone* who does not receive Jesus, now that we live in this post-resurrection era.

There is now no difference between Jew and Gentile. Yet we might observe a distinction: the gospel is to the Jew first and *then* to the Gentile. It is not that there is any status difference between Jew and Gentile; there is no hierarchy of favouritism in God's heart. In the UK as we speak about our political settlement and our governing powers, we speak of the Prime Minister and the Cabinet. The prime minister is only the "prime" minister but is recognized as being "first among equals" in the Cabinet. Perhaps that is a useful analogy of the position of Jew and non-Jew in God's household. In reality and at all strict jurisprudential levels there is no difference – we are equal. But at the practical level the Jew is first amongst equals. God will search for disciples first amongst His ethnic Chosen People and only then amongst His chosen people from every tribe and tongue. I offer up these thoughts only to add depth to the reality of the First Fruits. The Moedim collectively point to every aspect of Jesus' life, mission, ministry and return. Jesus is the first fruits of the resurrection, but this truth can be explored and understood at more than one level.

Notes
[1] See Further Reading section at the end of this book: Of all the studies on the Moedim known to this author, Daniel Fuchs' book is the most useful and is recommended on that basis.
[2] Op Cit, pages 32-33
[3] See Select Bibliography.

Chapter 8

LATTER FIRST FRUITS (ETERNAL HARVEST)

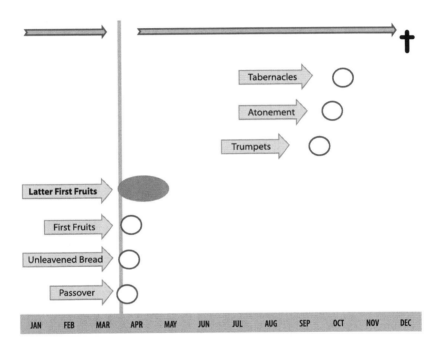

" 'From the day after the Sabbath, the day you brought the sheaf of the wave offering, count off seven full weeks. Count off fifty days up to the day after the seventh Sabbath, and then present an offering of new grain to the LORD. From wherever you live, bring two loaves made of two-tenths of an ephah of the finest flour, baked with yeast, as a wave offering of first fruits to the LORD.

Present with this bread seven male lambs, each a year old and without defect, one young bull and two rams. They will be a burnt offering to the LORD, together with their grain offerings and drink offerings — a food offering, an aroma pleasing to the LORD. Then sacrifice one male goat for a sin offering and two lambs, each a year old, for a fellowship offering.

The priest is to wave the two lambs before the LORD as a wave offering, together with the bread of the first fruits. They are a sacred offering to the LORD for the priest. On that same day you are to proclaim a sacred assembly and do no regular work. This is to be a lasting ordinance for the generations to come, wherever you live. " 'When you reap the harvest of your land, do not reap to the very edges of your field or gather the gleanings of your harvest. Leave them for the poor and for the foreigner residing among you. I am the LORD your God.' "

(Leviticus 23:15-22).

Meaning

In Appendix 2 we list the main alternative names associated with the seven Moedim. This Moed of *Latter First Fruits* is better known amongst Jewish people as Shavuot. Amongst Christians it is often known as Pentecost and remembered by them for two reasons: (1) as the first outpouring of the Holy Spirit upon disciples of Jesus; (2) as a putative beginning for the "Christian" church. Whilst there is a modicum of justification for both ideas, the true meaning of Latter First Fruits is altogether more exciting!

Let us revert to First Fruits for a moment: the meaning of that Moed is to allow the Hebrew nation to offer to God the first fruits of their spring harvest. That offering was a trivial token in terms of quantity, but it acknowledged that the whole harvest – including the anticipated summer and autumn harvest, in fact belongs to God. When we come to Latter First Fruits this is the climax of Israel's grain harvest, as it is the "first fruits" of the later anticipated harvest. Wheat goes on growing during the summer months and is not finally and fully harvested (or "white unto harvest" in the words of Jesus) until the seventh month. These are indeed the hot summer months.

The beginning of the grain harvest was marked by the 'sacrifice' of the "omer" – the first sheaf of newly cut barley, at First Fruits. Fifty days later, at the end of the First Fruits harvest period *two loaves* of bread, baked from the wheat of the new crop, were offered as a 'sacrifice' of praise. We note again that the number of loaves (two) was trivial in terms of the quantity of the anticipated harvest – again we can say that the primary symbolic significance of this offering was to acknowledge that the entire anticipated harvest actually belongs to God. The two loaves were seen as a peace offering during the Temple era. A sin-offering preceded the peace offering. The peace offering was a heartfelt *thank-offering* for the people *who have peace with the Lord.* The *peace offering* of Latter First Fruits was symbolically a meal of fellowship and peace between God and His redeemed people. As we shall see shortly, however, there is a deeper theological significance to the two loaves offered at Latter First Fruits as opposed to the single loaf offered at First Fruits....

Prophetic Fulfilment

The Lord Jesus, as we have seen, is the First Fruits – He is the first to be resurrected and His resurrection is the first part of a much greater harvest. Judaism traditionally marked a thanksgiving to God for their early harvest, *trusting in a later harvest*. The first fruits have of course already been offered. The implicit promise is that the latter harvest will also be safely gathered in – but prophetically this will be a harvest of souls, of those who are disciples of Israel's Messiah. Part of this latter harvest will be a large component of the Jewish people [cp. Romans 11:25-36] but numerically by far the greater component of this latter harvest will be those who are not Jewish, and yet have received Israel's Messiah as Lord and as Saviour.[1]

In the Latter First Fruits period, no longer will mankind "walk" by commandments given in tablets of stone, but instead by the power of the indwelling Holy Spirit, poured out at Shavuot (Latter First Fruits). We can go further and say that every believer in Jesus must have their Shavuot moment, when the Holy Spirit first indwells them.

Present Jewish Observance

Since the destruction of the Temple in AD70, Shavuot has progressively "evolved" within the Rabbinic tradition. It is believed by Rabbinic Jews that Shavuot coincides with the giving of the Law to Moses.

Modern observance, then, has morphed to become a celebration of Torah. Spiritually, it seems, Rabbinic Judaism has retreated inwards to a celebration of the "Law", instead of an acknowledgement of the *one* who has fulfilled that Law for all mankind. It has become an inward looking affirmation of the Torah (teaching) rather than an outward focused celebration of how the Torah (teaching) will bless the entire world, as a vast harvest of souls will be gathered into God's store room. This loss of meaning for Jews is a real tragedy.

The modern Rabbinic equivalent of Latter First Fruits (Shavuot) incorporates the ritual of "counting the omer". The precise instruction in Leviticus 23:16 is to count off fifty days, and on the fiftieth day to present a new grain offering. Read straightforwardly, this simply means to allow seven weeks to elapse and then to mark the Latter First Fruits Moed; however the modern Rabbinic ritual is to mark-off (or count) *each individual day* and to incorporate special prayers for each day. Again this adds considerable religious ritual, but no assurance and (apparently) no joy – except perhaps for those who do the counting and praying correctly.

Re: Jesus

The Lord Jesus, having fulfilled the "type" of the Passover lamb at Calvary, when the corn of wheat was metaphorically placed in the ground (buried at the feast of Unleavened Bread), rose from the dead to become the "first fruits", fulfilling the "type" of the wave sheaf. Fifty days later, the Holy Spirit is poured out on believers in a dramatic new way, underlining the inauguration of the New Covenant [Acts 1:5 and Acts 2:1-2]. (The institutional church traditionally calls this "Pentecost" – this word being derived from the Greek for "fifty"). After the *Latter First Fruits* feast (or Pentecost), God's holy laws are written directly onto men's hearts, and the Spirit of Jesus – the Holy Spirit – comes to indwell all who are His true disciples.

Why do the Hebrew people offer *two loaves* as part of their end of harvest celebration? Could it be that there is an emblematic significance to the two that is lost upon Rabbinic Judaism? Could it be that the two loaves represent two communities of believers offered to God? Firstly, Jewish believers in Yeshua, and secondly, the non-Jewish believers in Yeshua? God's family of true believers was always going to be drawn from all nations and all tongues (Revelation 7:9). These two sacrificial loaves are the *completed product* of two parallel harvests, but offered up to the same saving Father. Put another way, God's household was always going to be enlarged to encompass all humankind. The two that were formerly far apart are now unified before their God, as "One New Man" (Ephesians 2:14).

Commentary

We should note that Latter First Fruits is also, perhaps confusingly, known as the Feast of Weeks. Why is this, and is that important or in some way symbolic? We note that in Leviticus 23:16 the command is specific: **"Count off fifty days up to the day after the seventh Sabbath, and then present an offering of new grain to the LORD"**. We explore in Appendix 4 that the number seven is important to denote completion or perfection from God's viewpoint. The fifty days were in a very real sense *a week of weeks* (and if it does not sound a trite analogy in this serious context, in the UK we often speak of 'a month of Sundays', meaning a long, slow-moving or indeterminate period). So the fifty of 'Pentecost' is *a week of weeks* being seven times seven = 49 days, plus one day, when the holy convocation is to be marked. It is as if God is saying "this latter harvest, combined with the First Fruits, will be My perfect and complete harvest. There is nothing more to be gathered in". Harvesting is what Jesus is most interested in: we remember His command to His disciples: **"The harvest is plentiful, but the workers are few. Ask the Lord of the harvest, therefore, to send out workers into his harvest field"** (Luke 10:2; Matthew 9:38).

Shavuot presents a richer picture, and richer truths, than is typically understood by either the institutional church or by Rabbinic Judaism. The real truth is that from the time of Pentecost as recorded in the Acts of the Apostles, the harvest of believers has grown and grown – there is no limit to that growth except the willingness of individual people to turn to Jesus in faith and repentance. That is the limit! But what a wonderful truth this is. Readers who do not know Jesus as Lord and as Saviour can have confidence that there is a place in Jesus' Kingdom for them personally, and there is nothing that they have done, and no sin that they have committed that is unforgivable. Jesus has already paid the price of your sins! He has died in your place. Your task is simply to accept His free gift of salvation, and then to follow Him faithfully!

Many believe that the Latter First Fruits (Shavuot) period is, in reality, the whole of history from the time of the first incarnation of Jesus, until His second incarnation – which will be His return in glory. Some will call this the "church age" and there is a modicum of truth in that title. However, the term may be deeply misleading and possibly contributes (wittingly or unwittingly) to the profound error that is dubbed "Replacement Theology". Whilst the Bible does not give a "title" to this period beyond Latter First Fruits, we could perhaps suggest the following as a usable definition of this epoch: *the time of the Kingdom on Earth prior to the Lord's return in glory.*

We outline this Latter First Fruits period, in its *entirety*, in the following diagrams. The issues that these diagrams raise are complex and need to be worked through biblically and in prayer. They express, however, some profound truths in a relatively simple and straightforward manner, so it is hoped that readers find this useful as a starting point to pursue further study. Remember the outline of the seven Moedim are as follows:

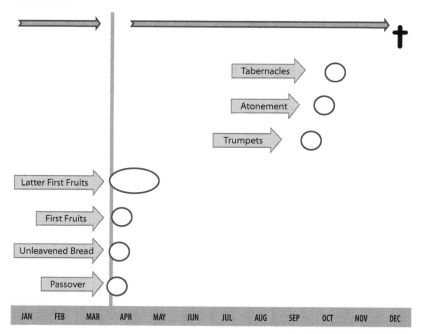

And remember that the underlying theme relates to the completed ministry of Yeshua ha Massiach (Jesus the Messiah) in the way indicated in the first diagram at the head of this chapter. How then do we define the Shavuot ("Latter First Fruits") period? Two definitions are possible and both are correct:

DEFINITION # 1: Jesus is the first fruits, being the second Adam and the initiator and the seal of the new covenant. The "latter first fruits" are all those early Jewish believers (and others) whose story is set out in the Acts of the Apostles, the epistles, and the apocalyptic Revelation. In this sense the Latter First Fruits are the early church, with the full harvest still to be gathered.

DEFINITION # 2: The "latter first fruits" are ALL those who trust in Jesus as Lord and as Saviour, from the book of Acts until Messiah's second incarnation (i.e. when Messiah returns in bodily form to this world). All of this period is, in effect, the Shavuot period. On our outline chart this can be depicted as follows:

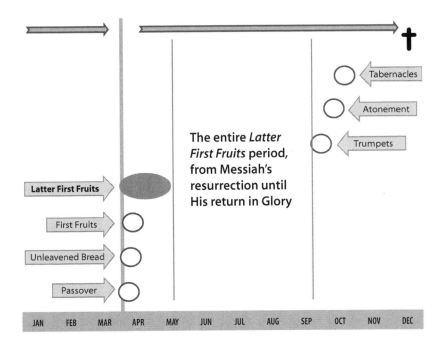

The book of Ruth is emblematic of this period. Ruth, a Gentile, met her kinsman redeemer and became an ancestor of King David and of Yeshua. She also speaks of those Gentiles who are graciously given the "right" to glean and gain sustenance (life) from the harvest. Any proper study of the Book of Ruth will uncover the spiritual truth that Ruth's romantic suitor is her "kinsman redeemer". Serious theologians recognise the kinsman redeemer as a "type" of Messiah, Whose task, as a member of the human race (and therefore a *kinsman*) is to redeem (buy-back) mankind at the cost of His own life. Ruth was a Moabitess and therefore a non-Jew. She is representative of all those non-Jews that are disciples of Jesus – and numerically this is by far the bulk of true believers. The Jewish nation remains today small, yet the numbers of disciples of the Lord Jesus has expanded down through history, and today accumulates to the hundreds of millions (or billions?). Non-Jews, it may be remembered, were generically not covered by the Old Testament covenants that we explored in chapter 2,[2] and so they needed to be grafted-in to spiritual Israel so as to be covered by those same promises. This has been likened to the symbolic "right" of *the poor* and *the alien* to "glean" sustenance at the edge of the field, where they could freely gather enough to sustain them. The Israelite farmers were not to harvest right up to the edge of the field, so leaving enough for the gleaners (Leviticus 19:9 and 23:22). If there are Christians who think the details of the book of Leviticus are "boring" then they should think again! Here are two instructions that affect each and every one of us; we are granted the right to "glean" at the edge of the Jewish field and to find "life" in those gleanings).[3]

Now this is a truth that may prick the pride of some Christians. The Apostle Paul in Romans chapter 11 refers obliquely to the Latter First Fruits in his otherwise rather obscure comment about "dough": **"I am talking to you Gentiles. Inasmuch as I am the apostle to the Gentiles, I take pride in my ministry in the hope that I may somehow arouse my own people to envy and save some of them. For if their rejection brought reconciliation to the world, what will their acceptance be but life from the dead? If the part of the dough offered as first-fruits is holy, then the whole batch is holy; if the root is holy, so are the branches.** (Romans 11:13-16). Here Paul is commenting on the mystery that the Jewish rejection of Jesus directly brings blessings to non-Jews.

Paul affirms that he wants to save "some of them" and elsewhere he prophesies that the majority of Jews will one day place their trust in Yeshua ha Massiach (Jesus the Messiah, or Jesus the Christ). So Paul says that, if the "first fruits" are holy (in this case the Jewish disciples of Jesus), so then the whole batch of dough will similarly be holy – and therefore acceptable to the Lord. These are complex questions and readers should not be too alarmed if they find this difficult to follow at first reading!

So the amazing good news contained collectively within God's Moedim is that there will be a harvest, both an early harvest and a late harvest – and it is eternal. There is much to consider and to marvel at in these truths, but hopefully we have encouraged you to explore this further. Let us conclude these thoughts with a little more detail from the instructions in Leviticus:

"From wherever you live, bring two loaves made of two-tenths of an ephah of the finest flour, baked with yeast, as a wave offering of first fruits to the Lord. Present with this bread seven male lambs, each a year old and without defect, one young bull and two rams. They will be a burnt offering to the Lord, together with their grain offerings and drink offerings—a food offering, an aroma pleasing to the Lord. Then sacrifice one male goat for a sin offering and two lambs, each a year old, for a fellowship offering"
(Leviticus 23:17-19).

We see here the reference to the *two loaves*, which we have already suggested are emblematic of Jewish and non-Jewish believers in Jesus, equal parts of one family. These were a fellowship offering, and so denote the 'peace' that exists between this family and their God. But why *two lambs* for slaughter? We reflect that the Latter First Fruits instructions in the verses above are analogous to the Passover meal – bread and lamb. The two lambs then are emblematic of the sacrifice of Jesus equally for two groups of human beings, first those who are Jewish and second those who are non Jewish, but now both united as a single family. Hallelulia!

As we reflect upon this Latter First Fruits period we must also acknowledge that this period reaches a climax – harvest! There is a time for sowing and reaping. If we can say that the church has a primary mission – indeed a sole mission – it is to sow and then to reap. That is what this Moed teaches us. Of course, spiritually this Moed is extended until the return of the Messiah – and assuming that Jesus was crucified and raised in approximately AD26 then we are approaching the anniversary of two thousand years of this harvest season – indeed two thousand years of the time when non Jews ("Gentiles") may glean at the allegorical "edges" of the Jewish field, but as with Ruth the Moabitess, our Kinsman Redeemer is glad to adopt us to be a part of His chosen family. Hallelulia!

Much of the Christian church has chosen to call this Moed of Latter First Fruits "Pentecost" and has focused upon the pouring out of the Holy Spirit in Acts chapter 2. This is a valid focus and indeed the Greek word used in the text is indeed Pentecost, being fifty (that is, forty-nine plus one, as we have already seen). However that is a Greek interpolation; the people of Jesus' day did not in reality say "this is the day of fifty" or "this is the day of forty nine plus one"! That is why in the One New Man Translation the Hebrew word Shavuot is used instead of Pentecost. Whilst I think this is both technically correct and valid, the Greek word is "fifty" so I am content to use that term in this context. So where in Acts chapter 2 we read that the Spirit was poured out on Pentecost, we should really make the mental adjustment to "the Spirit was poured out on Latter First Fruits". This makes perfect sense, as the gift of the Spirit poured out was (and is!) *the* necessary empowerment needed by Jesus' disciples to live and to witness and to work in what would quickly become[4] the post Second Temple and post Levitical priesthood world of the new covenant.

As the apostle Peter addressed the crowd at Latter First Fruits ("Pentecost") on that wonderful day he quoted from the prophet Joel (Acts 2:17-21), that "in the last days" God would "pour out His Spirit" on all people, male and female, young and old. And that is precisely what God has done. These days in which we live today and in which we have been living since the ascension of Jesus are in a very real sense "the latter days" – they are the days leading up directly to the return of the Lord announced by a Trumpet blast. Once again, we have to exclaim "Hallelulia!"

Notes

[1] It is challenging to understand, let alone to summarise, the prophetic meaning(s) of First Fruits and Latter First Fruits, as they can be interpreted with several layers of meaning. The First Fruits is at the beginning of the barley harvest. The Latter First Fruits is at the end of the barley harvest and the beginning of the wheat harvest, which extends throughout the summer months. It is not difficult to see how this apparently trivial distinction may have a much deeper theological significance.

[2] Gentiles (as heathens) were able to come into covenant relationship if they were willing to become proselytes (cf Exodus 12:48). This is an important matter to note: Israel became exclusivist and exclusionary, though this was never the Lord's intention, just as the institutional church has become exclusivist in its Replacement Theology and its signal failure to understand the reality on ONE NEW MAN (Ephesians 2:15).

[3] No wonder in another context, the Apostle Paul reminded Gentile believers not to be proud but to remember that they do not support the root, but that the root supports them! (Romans 11:18)

[4] The destruction of the Temple occurred in AD70.

Chapter 9

TRUMPETS (SECOND COMING)

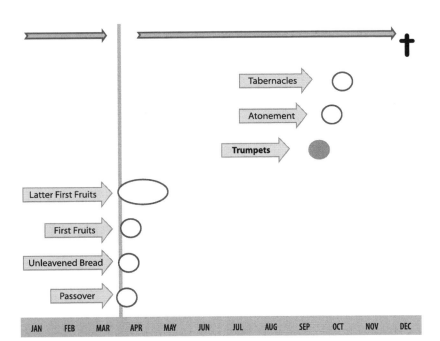

The LORD said to Moses, "Say to the Israelites: 'On the first day of the seventh month you are to have a day of sabbath rest, a sacred assembly commemorated with trumpet blasts. Do no regular work, but present a food offering to the LORD.' "

(Leviticus 23:23-25)

Meaning

The seventh month was in Biblical times, and remains today, especially holy to observant Jews. It was particularly sacred because of its association with the hallowed cycle of sevens; as we have seen the number seven is associated with completion or with perfection.[1] In this seventh month of Tishrei occur the three most holy Moedim. Atonement is still recognized as the most holy day of the Jewish year, and it is 'flanked' by Trumpets and by Tabernacles – there is, in the Rabbinic Jewish consciousness, a sort of *holy trinity* around these three Moedim. They very much represent the completion of God's holy salvation purposes. From the perspective of the Biblical Moedim, the future of mankind and the consummation of all things occur in this seventh month of Tishrei.

We turn to Leviticus 23:23 – 25. Yom Teruah (the day of trumpets) is a re-gathering of the people. They are re-gathered *because* of the earlier and completed work of the Messiah:

- *Passover* – Messiah's sacrifice
- *Unleavened Bread* – Messiah's holiness imparted to those who "feed" on Him, together with the Lord's burial as the crucified One, Who will see no decay
- *First Fruits* – those Hebrew people who first trusted in Messiah and placed their faith in His completed work on the cross of crucifixion
- *Latter First Fruits* – those Gentile people who place their faith in Yeshua, the Jewish Messiah

Trumpets represents the re-gathering of two distinct but linked groups: Firstly, the re-gathering of Jewish people generally within the biblical *Promised Land*; secondly, the final gathering of all people, Jews and non-Jews, who are true believers at the time of the end. Why are they re-gathered? (1) So that they can assemble before their Lord and worship Him; (2) So that they can reign with Him.

Prophetic Fulfilment

How awful that day will be! No other will be like it. It will be a time of trouble for Jacob, but he will be saved out of it. (Jeremiah 30:7)

"At that time Michael, the great prince who protects your people, will arise. There will be a time of distress such as has not happened from the beginning of nations until then. But at that time your people — everyone whose name is found written in the book — will be delivered (Daniel 12:1).

This is not a book about the end times and readers who want to dig deeper into this complex subject will find material published both in books and online. Your author would caution his readers concerning two things: (1) some of the interpretations of end-time events are wacky, and (2) some of the interpretations encompass mutually exclusive views, and tend to pit Christians against each other. However, it is clear from the Bible and from the words of Jesus that there will be an end time, and that following this there will be a judgement. The issues on which most Christians can agree are summarised in the book *The Bible Student* which is freely available study by study on the website: www.christian-publications-int.com and in its study number 44 *The Second Coming*.

The Moed of Trumpets characterises a time of in-gathering and spiritual preparation. There are numerous biblical promises of a time of *complete shalom* for the Chosen People in their Promised Land. Since no such time has happened in the past, it is reasonable to conclude that it lies in the future. Prior to the *completion* of that re-gathering, there is a metaphorical trumpet call (strictly speaking a Shofar call) to the Hebrew people globally to "come home".

Whether there will be some additional supernatural "call" specifically to Jewish people remains to be seen.[2]

Finally there will be an equivalent "trumpet call" to the whole of mankind to place their faith and trust in the Jewish Messiah. In spite of widespread and very severe persecution against true believers, yet people will continue to turn to Jesus until the very end – when He returns in Glory.

Present Jewish Observance

Rabbinic Judaism no longer marks Trumpets. Instead it has substituted Rosh Hashanah (the "new year"). There is a Jewish cultural/traditional motif that, on Rosh Hashanah, God judges the world. Between Rosh Hashanah and Atonement it is supposed that there should be good deeds and prayers – but no assurance of forgiveness is possible.

It has been observed that Rosh Hashanah is a sad mixture of biblical truth and paganism, with a special debt owed to the ancient Babylonian Marduk "room of fate". The idea of repentance is also bound up in the Rabbinical traditions. Rosh Hashanah to the Rabbis represents the "spiritual" new year.

Re: Jesus

Biblically, the Shofar was to be blown as an announcement of God's Moedim – His holy convocations with His people. Whilst these Moedim describe His relationship with His *chosen people*, there is a direct transference of significance to all those who place their faith in Yeshua – those grafted in to the root of Israel [Romans 10:5-13; Romans 11:24]. Numbers 10 lists a range of occasions when a metal trumpet was to be blown.[3] It seems that this would be a sound distinctly different to the normative Shofar (always an animal's horn), so would not cause confusion as to what type of signal was being given.

The allusion to Messiah and His achievements through "Trumpets" is compelling. It seems that in some way the future global reign of Messiah will be announced with a trumpet blast [Revelation 11:15-17; 1 Thessalonians 4:16]. In summary, we can say that the feast of Trumpets is an allusion to the second coming of Messiah: **"And he will send his angels with a loud trumpet call, and they will gather his elect from the four winds, from one end of the heavens to the other"** (Matthew 24:31).

Commentary

The trumpet blast throughout Scripture is in itself always an announcement of great portent. After the long silence of the summer months when the harvest is developing and diligently and quietly being gathered, so at long last that silence is broken as a wonderful announcement is made:

the *Sabbath rest* has arrived! For believers, this is the physical return of the Saviour of the world. He is no longer the suffering servant. Now He is the judge of all mankind and the spiritual accountancy books must be opened! God knows those matters which must be judged, and how He will judge. All people face the judgement, yet some will be acquitted – not because there is insufficient evidence against them, and not because of personal merit. Rather they will be acquitted because God "sees" the penitent sinner through the blood of His Lamb. Christians speak of *being washed in the blood of the Lamb*, a term suggested by Revelation 7:14. In practical terms *washed in the blood*, means to have one's sins forgiven through the sacrifice of Jesus the Messiah. When He died on the cross, He was the Lamb of God, to be slaughtered like the Passover Lamb. Jesus made payment for mankind's sins once and for all, so that all who believe on Him might have forgiveness of their sins. It is sometimes commented that to be washed in water means natural bathing which cleans only the outside – but not the heart. Washed in water can also be an allusion to the act of baptism, but when we are baptized we are, in a very real sense, simultaneously "washed" in the blood of the Lamb (1 John 1:7).

"These are they who have come out of the great tribulation; they have washed their robes and made them white in the blood of the Lamb". (Revelation 7:14). Whilst the allusion in Revelation is to those who have come out of the Great Tribulation, there is a sense in which the entire Latter First Fruits period, in the harvesting months preceding Trumpets, is a period of trouble for Jesus' disciples. Jesus was quite clear that **"in this world you will have trouble"** (John 16:33) because we are His disciples. He said **"You will be hated by everyone because of me, but the one who stands firm to the end will be saved"** (Matthew 10:22). Indeed the Lord's warnings about sufferings and persecutions are sober and solemn warnings (see Mark 13:3-13; Matthew 24:3-14; Luke 21:5-6).

As Greg Stevenson says in his booklet: "The primary functions of the Shofar are as a method of proclamation, of alarm, as a warning, or as an instrument of praise and prayer." Stevenson goes on to list no fewer than sixteen occasions when the Shofar was blown in Biblical times, of which the last three that he notes are:

14. In the future, during the great tribulation – the time of Jacob's Trouble;

15. As an expression of hope for the coming Messiah and the resurrection;

16. At Yeshua's return (1 Thessalonians 4:16; 1 Corinthians 15:52).

Taken in context with the preceding four Moedim, there can be no serious doubt that the Lord Jesus will return at the Moed of Trumpets. Our knowledge of the Holy Day of Trumpets and how it was celebrated in Biblical times is quite limited. According to Alfred Edersheim, trumpets and horns were blown in Jerusalem from morning to evening. these would not be the metal trumpets of the priests, but rather the horns of animals. Most frequently the ram's horn would be used, which is especially redolent of our Jesus theme when we reflect that when Abraham was poised to sacrifice his only son, he looked up **"and saw a ram caught in bush by its horns. He went and got it and offered it as a burnt offering instead of his son"** (Genesis 22:13, GNT).

The prophetic significance of Trumpets is that the long period of harvest will be ended. As we noted earlier, we are now close to two thousand years of the harvest period, and we know that it will not extend forever. Millions from every nation, tribe and tongue have gleaned in the fields during these summer months, down through those two thousand years. The First Fruits have been harvested. The harvesting of the Latter First Fruits now approaches its climax: **"Listen, I tell you a mystery: We will not all sleep, but we will all be changed – in a flash, in the twinkling of an eye, at the last trumpet. For the trumpet will sound, the dead will be raised imperishable, and we will be changed"** (1 Corinthians 15:51-52). The fields, as Jesus said, are ripe unto harvest. One day the summer will end and the silence of those long months will be over, concluded with a trumpet blast! Many believers are today quietly confident that the next event in God's prophetic eternal calendar is The Feast of Trumpets – the return of the Lord.[4]

Notes

[1] See Appendix 4

[2] Many believe that the Aliyah of Jews to Israel is a precursor to the End Time. This has been underway since the mid nineteenth century and continues to our own day. At the time of writing French Jews are making Aliyah in greater numbers as France becomes increasingly hostile to Jews. Is this a shofar blast?

[3] Greg Stevenson in his excellent booklet "The Message of the Shofar – and its application to believers through the Feasts of the Lord" (published by CMJ in the UK in 2013) comments that the two metal trumpets of Numbers 10 may be an allusion to two different groups called to God's presence – Jews and non Jews. In the light of our discussion in relation to Latter First Fruits and the two loaves and the two Lambs, I concur with his view.

[4] Some Christians say it is heresy to purport to know, or presume to know, the timing of the Lord's return and will quote Matthew 24:36 to support their view. It would require a full additional chapter to open up this subject and probably a full book to explore it satisfactorily, however we should note carefully that the Lord Jesus gave a number of prophetic signs as to the timing of His own return [at least ten in Matthew chapter 24 alone] and commanded that His disciples should be alert, looking for the imminency of His return. Whilst not definitive, the web-based resources below may provide additional and useful perspective on this question:

http://christianitybeliefs.org/end-times-deceptions/no-one-knows-the-day-and-hour-of-jesus-return/

http://www.hebroots.org/hebrootsarchive/9807/980715_c.html

Your author's view is that it is likely that the Lord will return at the Moed of Trumpets, *year unknown*. Failing that, the next likely candidate would be Tabernacles, but noting that a mere fourteen days separate these two Moeds! We can be reasonably assured then, as to the time of year – if not the year itself.

Chapter 10

ATONEMENT
(FORGIVENESS AND NEW LIFE)

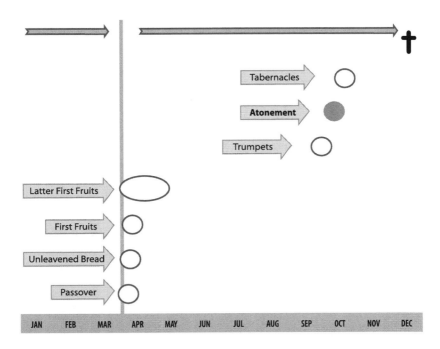

The LORD said to Moses, "The tenth day of this seventh month is the Day of Atonement. Hold a sacred assembly and deny yourselves, and present a food offering to the LORD.

Do not do any work on that day, because it is the Day of Atonement, when atonement is made for you before the LORD your God. Those who do not deny themselves on that day must be cut off from their people. I will destroy from among their people anyone who does any work on that day. You shall do no work at all. This is to be a

lasting ordinance for the generations to come, wherever you live. It is a day of Sabbath rest for you, and you must deny yourselves. From the evening of the ninth day of the month until the following evening you are to observe your Sabbath."

(Leviticus 23:26-32)

"On the tenth day of this seventh month hold a sacred assembly. You must deny yourselves and do no work. Present as an aroma pleasing to the LORD a burnt offering of one young bull, one ram and seven male lambs a year old, all without defect. With the bull offer a grain offering of three-tenths of an ephah of the finest flour mixed with oil; with the ram, two-tenths; and with each of the seven lambs, one-tenth. Include one male goat as a sin offering, in addition to the sin offering for atonement and the regular burnt offering with its grain offering, and their drink offerings".

(Numbers 29:7-11)

Meaning

The Day of Atonement, set out as God's command for His people in Leviticus 23:26-32, was the most solemn of all the Moedim, occurring once a year on the tenth day of Tishrei, the seventh month of the Hebrew calendar. On that day the High Priest would perform specific rituals to atone for the sins of the people. First described in Leviticus 16:1-34, the atonement ritual began with Aaron, and would subsequently be observed by other High Priests of Israel, by their coming into the holy of holies, into the very presence of God. The seriousness of the ritual was underscored by God telling Moses to warn Aaron not to come into the Most Holy Place whenever he felt like it, but only on this special day once a year, lest he die (16:2). This was a ceremony not to be taken lightly, and the people needed to understand that atonement for sin must be done in God's way.

During their years of wandering in the desert, the Israelites worshiped God through the Tabernacle system, which later became the Temple system. Before entering the Tabernacle, Aaron was to bathe and put on special garments (16:4), then sacrifice a bull for a sin offering for himself and his family (16: 6 and 11). The blood of the bull was to be sprinkled on the Ark of the Covenant. Aaron was then to bring two goats, one to be sacrificed "because of the uncleanness and rebellion of the Israelites, whatever their sins have been" (16:16, NIV), and its blood was sprinkled on the Ark of the Covenant. The other goat was used as the *scapegoat*. Aaron placed his hands on the scapegoat's head, made confession over it for the sins of the Israelites, and then banished the goat, which would be accompanied by a man who would release it into the wilderness (16:21). The goat symbolically carried on itself all the sins of the people, who were forgiven for another year (16:30). It would perish "outside the camp" (see Leviticus 16:26).

Why a goat instead of a lamb, as in Passover? We cannot perhaps offer a definitive view on this, but it can be said that whereas a lamb is known for its gentleness and willingness to follow, goats are by comparison headstrong and strong willed. In this sense they are a more obvious "type" of a sinner – because sin is ultimately a refusal to follow and a demand to go our own way. That is what goats tend to do! But the importance of the Day of Atonement has little to do with the genus of the animal sacrificed. It is far more about truthful acknowledgement and heartfelt sorrow for sin, and recognition that only the High Priest could make sacrifice for the people. He could do that only once a year, and then only through the observance of very strict regulations.

Prophetic Fulfilment

A new and better sacrifice was required. It is ironic that before offering the sacrifice for the people, the priest had to offer a sacrifice *for his own sins*! The more correctly the letter of the Law was observed on the Day of Atonement, the more eloquently it testified that the Law is "weak" and "useless" and a better hope was required [Hebrews 10:1-2]. The letter to the Hebrews is a wonderful explanation of the Day of Atonement, clearly showing the shortcomings of the Law. It is a commentary on Romans 8:3-4. **"It is impossible for the blood of bulls and goats to take away sins"** [Hebrews 10:4]. How much better is Yeshua, our great High Priest! He achieves what no Levitical priest could ever do. As a man He was without sin – Yeshua did not have to offer a sacrifice for His sin. He was able to offer His sinless human life as a sin offering for others. Because He is both God *and* Man, He is both priest and victim.

As the One who conquered death, He offers Himself as our atonement on the cross of crucifixion.

Present Jewish Observance

Yom Kippur is the most holy day in the Jewish biblical calendar. Historically the Day of Atonement was *the* day once a year when the High Priest entered the Holy of Holies to atone for his own sins and for the sins of the people (see Leviticus 16). Today Rabbinical Judaism has no Temple and no Levitical priesthood – no way, in fact, to "keep" this eternal command. The day is still marked, even by some secular Jews, as a cultural statement. It has become simply a day of fasting and religious reflection, a seeking of forgiveness from judgement for sins against G-d, but it carries no assurance – because the scriptural ordinances can no longer be fulfilled. In marking the annual Day of Atonement, which falls on different days each year in September–October, many Jews will traditionally observe the holy day with a 25-hour period of fasting and intensive prayer, often spending most of the day in synagogue services.

Re: Jesus

The epistle to the Hebrews contrasts our High Priest Jesus, with the High Priest of Israel [Hebrews 7:22-27]. The Day of Atonement demonstrated the truth that all the sacrifices of the Law could not provide an eternal solution to the problem of sin. At best, it could only deal with the sins of the previous year! Only the Lord Yeshua, Israel's Eternal High Priest, can say **"I give them eternal life, and they shall never perish; no one can snatch them out of My hand"** [John 10:28]. See Hebrews 8:1-2: Jesus is now the true High Priest, and He is a holy High Priest. Jesus' life after death, evidenced by the resurrection, is *the* guarantee that He imparts that same life to His true disciples. Our sins are atoned for. We *are* forgiven. Praise God!

The symbolic significance of the Levitical ritual, particularly to Christians, is identified first in the washing and cleansing of the High Priest, as well as the man who released the goat, and the man who took the sacrificed animals outside the camp to burn their carcasses (see Leviticus 16:4, 24, 26, 28). Israelite washing ceremonies were required throughout the Old Testament period and symbolised the need for people to be cleansed of sin. But it was not until Jesus came to make the "once for all" sacrifice that the need for cleansing ceremonies ceased (Hebrews 7:27). The blood of bulls and goats could only atone for sins if the ritual was continually done year after year, whilst the Messiah's sacrifice was sufficient for all the sins of all who would ever believe in Him. When His sacrifice was made, He declared, "It is finished" (John 19:30). He then sat down at the right hand of God, and no further sacrifice would ever be needed (Hebrews 10:1-12).

Commentary

Yom Kippur has long been considered as the most holy day in the Jewish biblical calendar. How can Rabbinic Jews mark this holy convocation without the proper place for sacrifice? The rabbis of the Second Century decided to create substitutes to fill the gap. *Tefilah* (prayer), *Teshuvah* (repentance) and *Tzedakah* (charity) replace animal sacrifice in the modern observance of the Day of Atonement. There remains a double tragedy in this rabbinic observance: plainly it creates a man-made "solution" to the "problem" of there being no Temple and no Priesthood – or indeed High Priest – to intercede for the people. Secondly it masks the fact that Atonement has *already been made* for the sins of the people *for all time*. "**........ Jesus has become the guarantor of a better covenant. Now there have been many of those priests, since death prevented them from continuing in office; but because Jesus lives forever, he has a permanent priesthood. Therefore he is able to save completely those who come to God through him, because he always lives to intercede for them. Such a high priest truly meets our need – one who is holy, blameless, pure, set apart from sinners, exalted above the heavens. Unlike the other high priests, he does not need to offer sacrifices day after day, first for his own sins, and then for the sins of the people. He sacrificed for their sins once for all when he offered himself**".

(Hebrews 7:22-27)

We can say that Atonement is the act by which God and man are brought together in personal and permanent relationship. The word in English is derived from Anglo-Saxon words meaning "making at one".

Hence "at-one-ment". It presupposes a separation – indeed alienation – that must be overcome if humans are to know God and have fellowship with Him. The word atonement is translated from the Old Testament "Kaphar" – to cover – meaning that sins have been *covered over* by the blood of the Sacrifice, and that the sinner and God have become "at one". In theology, the word atonement has come to include the whole idea of redemption through the blood of the Messiah. The word is used once in the New Testament, in Romans 5:11 (Authorised Version) but tends in modern translations to be translated as "reconciliation" which is possibly a clearer word in the modern language.

The need for atonement, or reconciliation, is bound up with man's thorough addiction to sin. All of Scripture points to our sin, for examples:

Isaiah 53:6 – all we like sheep have gone astray
Jeremiah 17:9 – the heart is deceitful above all things, and desperately corrupt, who can understand it?
Psalm 14:3 – there is none that do good, no, not one
Romans 3:23 – all have sinned and fall short of the glory of God

The apostle Paul described men as "enemies of God" (Rom 5:10), "hostile to God" (Rom 8:7) and "estranged and hostile in mind" (Col 1:21)

In Old Testament times, sins were covered by God in anticipation of the Cross. That was the purpose of the Day of Atonement. Sacrifice was the remedy for sin, and a man would sacrifice not only for his own sins but also for the sins of his family. Having truly repented, he would sacrifice an innocent animal – and always an animal without blemish. He trusted that God would fulfil His promise by cleaning him from his sin, if he offered blood.

Ex 30:10
Heb 10:4
Lev 1:3-4; 4:27-31
Lev 16:11, 17, 30; 17:11; 23:27

It is reasonably straightforward to see that animal sacrifices of first and second Temple Judaism *were in anticipation of the Sacrifice of Jesus* – they were in a very real sense "shadows" of which Messiah's sacrificial death was the reality. These texts help us to see this more clearly:

Heb 10:1
John 1:29
1 John 2:2
Heb 9:13-15, 22, 26; 10:10, 14
Rom 3:25
Rom 8:3
1 Cor 5:7

Today, under grace, having repented of sins, and having faith in the blood of Jesus shed for us, we are reconciled to God. Atonement has been made, once and for all. Reconciliation has been achieved through the blood of Jesus. His blood was *the* necessary price to be paid for the redemption and atonement of the world. It is really no exaggeration, then, to say that Christ's death was the supreme moment, the supreme event, in the history of the world.

Mark 10:45
John 10:11
Rom 3:21-25
Rom 5:10, 11
2 Cor 5:21
Eph 1:7
1 Peter 1:18-19
1 John 4:10

The day of Atonement, as we have seen, fits in perfectly with the clear theme of the seven Moedim. Jesus, having returned to this world (at Trumpets)[1] communes with those "covered by the blood", who find both forgiveness and new life forever. But the reality of Trumpets and Atonement taken together remind us that *there is a judgment that accompanies the glorious return of Jesus*. Some will be inside the camp, as it were, and washed in the blood of the sacrifice. Yet many others will be outside the camp, having rejected both the sacrifice and the Holy God Who sent the sacrifice. **"How shall we escape if we ignore such a great salvation?"** asked the writer to the Hebrews (Hebrews 2:3).

Finally, there are three terms that will be helpful to us in understanding *the* Atonement, and, if we may put it this way – to understand its "legal" rigour. They are:

Representative – Jesus' death was representative, see Hebrews 2:14-17 and Romans 5:19.
Propitiatory – Jesus' death makes of us what would otherwise be quite impossible – it makes us acceptable to God. (1 John 4:10)
Vicarious – Jesus' death was a substitute, because He died in our place – in the place of the repentant sinner (see Isaiah 53:5-6, and 1 Peter 2:24)

The completeness and sufficiency of the sacrifice of Messiah Jesus is reflected in the two goats; the blood of the first goat was sprinkled on the Ark of the Covenant, ritually appeasing the wrath of God for a further year. The second goat removed the sins of the Israelites and took them into the wilderness where they were forgotten and no longer tainted the people. For mankind taken as a whole, sin is both *propitiated* and *expiated* in God's way – only through the sacrifice of His Son, the Messiah, on the cross of crucifixion. Propitiation is the act of appeasing the wrath of God, while expiation is the act of atoning for sin and removing it from the sinner. Propitiation and expiation are achieved simultaneously by the crucifixion of Messiah Jesus. When He sacrificed Himself on the cross, Jesus appeased God's righteous wrath against sin, taking that wrath upon Himself: **"Since we have now been justified by his blood, how much more shall we be saved from God's wrath through him!"** (Romans 5:9). The banishing of sin through the *scapegoat* was a living parable of the promise that God would remove our transgressions from us as far as the east is from the west (Psalm 103:12) and that He would remember them no more (Hebrews 8:12; 10:17).

Note
[1] Plainly this is an assumption, but one that seems eminently reasonable and plausible given the prophetic coherence of the Moedim.

Chapter 11

TABERNACLES (ETERNAL HOME)

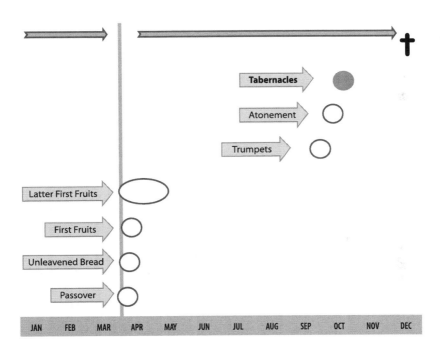

The LORD said to Moses, "Say to the Israelites: 'On the fifteenth day of the seventh month the LORD's Festival of Tabernacles begins, and it lasts for seven days. The first day is a sacred assembly; do no regular work. For seven days present food offerings to the LORD, and on the eighth day hold a sacred assembly and present a food offering to the LORD. It is the closing special assembly; do no regular work'."

"'These are the LORD's appointed festivals, which you are to proclaim as sacred assemblies for bringing food offerings to the LORD—the burnt offerings and grain offerings, sacrifices and drink offerings required for each day. These offerings are in addition to those for the LORD's Sabbaths and in addition to your gifts and whatever you have vowed and all the freewill offerings you give to the LORD.)

" 'So beginning with the fifteenth day of the seventh month, after you have gathered the crops of the land, celebrate the festival to the LORD for seven days; the first day is a day of sabbath rest, and the eighth day also is a day of Sabbath rest.

On the first day you are to take branches from luxuriant trees—from palms, willows and other leafy trees—and rejoice before the LORD your God for seven days. Celebrate this as a festival to the LORD for seven days each year. This is to be a lasting ordinance for the generations to come; celebrate it in the seventh month. Live in temporary shelters for seven days: All native-born Israelites are to live in such shelters so your descendants will know that I had the Israelites live in temporary shelters when I brought them out of Egypt. I am the LORD your God.' "

(Leviticus 23:33-43)

Meaning

The most joyful of Israel's feasts. It comes at the end of harvest, when crops are gathered and the people rejoice. As they look at the full harvest, people remember that six months previously they had dedicated the whole harvest to God ("First Fruits"). Pious Jews construct a tabernacle (or "booth", or "Sukkah") in which they and their family dwell during the feast, as a temporary reminder of earlier blessings. Tabernacles (or Sukkot) is an eight day feast, beginning and ending with a Sabbath. During the time of Jesus' earthly ministry the Sukkot included on each day a "libation of water" – a procession from the well at Siloam to the Jerusalem Temple. This was a symbolic act reminding the Jews of Isaiah 12:3.

Deuteronomy 16:13-17 adds depth to this Moed, especially the command for attendance at these specific feasts – Unleavened Bread, Latter First Fruits and Tabernacles, when "all your men" must appear before the Lord and bring some "gift" that reflects the way that God had already blessed them. Jewish men were required to take these Moedim very seriously. There will be a future counterpoint, or counterpart, to the ancient command for all men to appear before the Lord at Tabernacles, bearing a gift. This is set out in the book of Zechariah (see *Prophetic Fulfilment* immediately below).

Prophetic Fulfilment
All nations will be blessed through Israel (Genesis 12:3) and one day, in the future, Israel's ancient enemies will go up year by year to worship the Lord and to *celebrate the feast of Tabernacles* (Zechariah 14:16). In fact the whole of Zechariah chapter 14 describes this future time, so we can usefully pause at this point to read that chapter.

Tabernacles reminds us of the latter harvest, and of Israel's wilderness experience, when God dwelt with, and protected, His people in their forty-year temporary nomadic home. So today we are reminded that God faithfully watches over His people who presently live in a land that is not their true home (1 Peter 2:11). We are exiles living in a foreign land, and yet God is with us. Furthermore, He is coming again to live permanently with His people (Revelation 21:1-5), or perhaps we should more correctly say, He is coming again to *tabernacle permanently* with His true disciples.

Present Jewish Observance
Historically, Tabernacles *looks backwards* to the exodus when Israel lived in booths for forty years [Leviticus 23:42-43]. This reminds modern Jews of that time of exodus and also of the temporary nature of human existence. It also *looks forwards* to the future when God's promise to Abraham will be fulfilled – when "all nations will be blessed through you" (Genesis 12:3). Today, faithful Jews construct a Sukkah outside their home (sometimes inside if outside is impossible). Often a local synagogue will construct a Sukkah and incorporate this in some way into their services. We note, however, that the modern Jewish observance

is stuck in the past; it provides only a vague and uncertain hope for the future.

Tabernacles commemorates, then, the temporary booths (or huts) that the Israelites constructed in the wilderness. Sukkot is plural of the Hebrew Sukkah – so it is booths or huts – plural, the *common* and *shared* experience of the wandering Hebrew people in those 40 years. The walls of this structure were made of wood and the roof of twigs and greenery; literally the Israelites would be able to see the stars through these temporary structures. Some observant Jews today continue to sleep in these temporary structures during the eight day Tabernacles celebration; others use them primarily at meal times.

Re: Jesus
It is in John chapter 7 that we read of the Lord's teaching during this festival. The Good News Bible titles this "the Festival of Shelters" which is a perfectly good English title for Sukkot. In John 7:10-52 we read of the controversies around His ministry and the associated debates within Jerusalem, and how Jesus used the Taberncles Moed to point towards Himself – see especially 7:37-39, which we explore in the commentary below.

The primary understanding of Tabernacles for Christians is the eagerly anticipated return of Jesus to this world, to "tabernacle" with us. Most Christians recite the *Lord's Prayer* at least once a week, but often gloss over its first clause; "Thy kingdom come". This is the heartfelt call for a future, better, world where God's standards apply universally. In John 1:14 most translations of the Bible say that Jesus "dwelt" or "lived" amongst us, but the Greek word should optimally be translated as "tabernacled" – so Jesus tabernacled amongst us.[1] He will tabernacle with us again. If the Lord does not return at Trumpets (see chapter 9) then the Moed of Tabernacles could be a strong possibility. We must not try to be too definitive about this. What we can say with absolute assurance is that He *will* tabernacle with us, once again. That is certain.

Jesus the bridegroom will return for His bride [Matthew chapters 24 and 25 illustrate this]. Jesus will return. We must recognise that *The Word* or logos (Jesus/Yeshua) tabernacled amongst us [John 1:14], but in the future His abode with us will be permanent and everlasting [Daniel

7:13-14; Revelation chapter 21]. In the First Century observances, on Hoshana Rabba, the final day of Tabernacles, the daily "libation of water" ceremony reached its climax – when water was poured into a basin near the altar. Let us recall Jesus' attendance at that final Sukkot feast. As the Priest stood with an empty flask, a Man suddenly called out from the surrounding crowd: **"if anyone is thirsty, let him come to me and drink. Whoever believes in me as scripture has said, streams of living water will flow from within him"** [John 7:37-38; Proverbs 18: 4; Isaiah 58:11]. In saying this, Jesus was claiming that the miracle in the wilderness, when the rock gushed forth water, pointed to Himself! No wonder there was controversy about this itinerant preacher from Galilee!

Commentary

Indeed the Feast of Tabernacles was the most joyful of the Moedim. Coming at the end of harvest, the hearts of all Israelite people were naturally happy. Crops had been reaped, barns were full and people did not fear empty stomachs in the months ahead. Six months earlier, at First Fruits, they had dedicated the entire harvest to God. Now He had honoured their faithful dedication and provided that full harvest for which they had trusted Him. A pious Jew began his preparations for Tabernacles as soon as the Day of Atonement was finished. He had just five days in which to construct his Sukkah, in which he and his family would live during the eight day festival. Typically and by tradition, this temporary outdoor structure was to remind the Hebrews of their exodus wanderings, and of the transient nature of life itself. The roof was made of slats (or twigs and greenery) placed closely together so that the shade inside the Sukkah was more than the available light. The roof had to rest upon the walls, with no fastening. After that it would be "thatched" with green branches and the entire inside of the structure, including the ceiling, was decorated with fruit and flowers.

Tabernacles was the last of the three feasts when all adult males of ancient Israel came to and thronged Jerusalem.[2] In Deuteronomy 16:16-17 we read **"Three times a year all your men must appear before the LORD your God at the place he will choose: at the Festival of Unleavened Bread, the Festival of Weeks and the Festival of Tabernacles. No one should appear before the LORD empty-handed:**

each of you must bring a gift in proportion to the way the LORD your God has blessed you". So male attendance was a command of God.

Jesus dutifully kept this feast. One of the ceremonies of the Tabernacles festival was to bring water in a golden flask from the fountain of Siloam, to be poured into a basin near the altar. We need to recall that this ceremony was not a God-ordinance, and yet Jesus honoured the traditions of His time. The *Mishnah* says in Sukah 5:1 "he who has not seen the rejoicing at the place of the water drawing has never seen rejoicing in his life!" The ceremony was accompanied by dancing, singing, a torchlight procession and the chanting of the songs of ascents (Psalms 120-134). This was a symbolic ceremony carried out in compliance with Isaiah 12:3 **"with joy you will draw water from the wells of salvation".** We picture the scene: on the last and greatest day of Tabernacles (John 7:37), the crowds were in the Temple area, watching the white-robed priests on their ascent from Siloam to the Temple. The golden vase was before them, containing the water they had joyfully drawn from the well. Reaching the altar area, they poured out the precious fluid into the basin near the altar. Suddenly and unexpectedly, a Man shouts out with a loud voice, as John tells us: **"Jesus stood and said in a loud voice, "Let anyone who is thirsty come to me and drink. Whoever believes in me, as Scripture has said, rivers of living water will flow from within them."** These were challenging and audacious words! The whole point of the *libation of water ceremony* was to celebrate God's provision of life-giving water to the Hebrews as they faced death by dehydration in the desert. **"Let anyone who is thirsty come to me and drink".** In these words Jesus was claiming that this miracle in the book of Exodus, at the rock of Horeb,[3] pointed towards Himself. We recall Jesus' words in Revelation 21, which describes the future permanent feast of Tabernacles: **"To the thirsty I will give water without cost from the spring of the water of life".** This future consummation of Tabernacles makes for wonderful reading: **"And I heard a loud voice from the throne saying, "Look! God's dwelling place is now among the people, and he will dwell with them. They will be his people, and God himself will be with them and be their God. He will wipe every tear from their eyes. There will be no more death or mourning or crying or pain, for the old order of things has passed away."He**

**who was seated on the throne said, "I am making everything new!"
Then he said, "Write this down, for these words are trustworthy and
true." He said to me: "It is done. I am the Alpha and the Omega, the
Beginning and the End. To the thirsty I will give water without cost
from the spring of the water of life"** (Revelation 21:3-6).

Lastly, we can say that the Feast of Tabernacles is of particular interest
to Christians as it is the one – and only – feast that will be celebrated
by the nations of the world during the Millennial reign, that time when
Jesus rules the earth from Jerusalem. The book of Zechariah prophesies
that, in the Millennium, all nations will "go up" to Jerusalem for the
Feast of Tabernacles or bring God's wrath upon themselves if they refuse
to attend (Zechariah 14:16-19). The ultimate fulfilment of the Feast,
however, will arrive with the post-Millennial Kingdom of Jesus, when
God will once again "tabernacle" with His people, from every tribe and
tongue. It was on the final and greatest day of Tabernacles that Jesus
gave His promise of the Holy Spirit (John 7:39). As we read the whole
John chapter 7 we see the Lord's actions and teachings in the context
of enormous controversies that He was provoking, and which would
lead indirectly to His Crucifixion two years later. Readers may want to
pause at this point to read that chapter, and to try to get a sense of the
immensity of the emotions that Jesus was stirring.

Notes

[1] Some Bible commentators today opine that the Lord was born in the month of Tishrei
(September/October) to coincide with the Moed of Tabernacles – that He literally
"tabernacled among us", as in the original Greek wording of John 1:14. This makes
theological sense. We should note that Trumpets represents an equally strong (and
your author believes, stronger) candidate. We cannot, however, be definitive about this
subject which is, in any case, a secondary matter in terms of Kingdom theology and
God's holy purposes.

[2] Bible critics who deny the trustworthiness of the Jesus birth narratives sometimes
claim that the Romans would not have "troubled" to hold a census that required large
scale movement of people. These critics forget that in order to fulfil religious ceremony,
there were periods when people flocked in large numbers to Jerusalem, and Tabernacles
was just such an occasion! The prophetic evidence for a birth either at Trumpets or
Tabernacles is compelling, noting that a mere fourteen days separated these two feasts.

[3] Exodus 17:1-7

Chapter 12

THE ELEPHANT IN THE ROOM

Do We Comply Today?

As readers have worked through this book, it is likely that, irrespective of their background, they will have asked themselves the question, *Should we be observing these Feasts today, if we are disciples of the Lord Jesus*? This question requires a definitive and biblical answer and this Appendix seeks to provide it.

By way of background we should immediately recognise that there is a slowly growing interest within the broad church that refers to itself as the Jewish Roots Movement, or sometimes the Hebraic Roots Movement. Indeed this current goes under several names – we are merely mentioning the two most common. In general it reflects the desire of modern people to reconnect in some way with much of what has been lost of the Hebrew faith system that the Lord Jesus knew and which He loved, and which He honoured, that of Second Temple Judaism. Jesus honoured the Torah and said that He had not come to destroy the Torah, but to fulfil it [see Matthew 5:17-20].

"Think not that I am come to destroy the law, or the prophets: I am not come to destroy, but to fulfil. For verily I say unto you, Till heaven and earth pass, one jot or one tittle shall in no wise pass from the law, till all be fulfilled. Whosoever therefore shall break one of these least commandments, and shall teach men so, he shall be called the least in the kingdom of heaven: but whosoever shall do and teach them, the same shall be called great in the kingdom of heaven. For I say unto you, that except your righteousness shall exceed the righteousness of the scribes and Pharisees, ye shall in no case enter into the kingdom of heaven." (Matthew 5:17-20, KJV).

Whilst Jesus undoubtedly honoured both the Torah *and* the Prophets, He was simultaneously opposed to much of the "praxis" of the Temple system – with its burdensome "second law" and the hypocrisy with which the religious hierarchy "implemented" that Law. And so we see the growing controversy between Jesus and both the civil powers and the religious establishment, which had a mutual vested interest in the status quo and had no time for Jesus' vision of the Kingdom. Ultimately this unholy alliance of civil power and religious establishment would conspire to crucify Jesus. Several verses amongst many serve to show the Lord's condemnation, in particular, of the religious hierarchy:

Matt 15:1-3 "Then the scribes and Pharisees who were from Jerusalem came to Jesus, saying, "Why do Your disciples transgress the tradition of the elders? For they do not wash their hands when they eat bread." He answered and said to them, "Why do you also transgress the commandment of God because of your tradition?"

Matt 23:1-5 "Then Jesus spoke to the multitudes and to His disciples, saying: "The scribes and the Pharisees sit in Moses' seat. Therefore whatever they tell you to observe, that observe and do, but do not do according to their works; for they say, and do not do. For they bind heavy burdens, hard to bear, and lay them on men's shoulders; but they themselves will not move them with one of their fingers. But all their works they do to be seen by men."

Matt 23:31-33 "Therefore you are witnesses against yourselves that you are sons of those who murdered the prophets. Fill up, then, the measure of your fathers' guilt. Serpents, brood of vipers! How can you escape the condemnation of hell?"

Jesus continually reinforced His accusations against the religious establishment in their unwillingness to maintain a consistency between their tradition and the written law:

Matt 15:14 "They are blind leaders of the blind. And if the blind leads the blind, both will fall into a ditch."

Matt 23:13 "But woe to you, scribes and Pharisees, hypocrites! For you shut up the kingdom of heaven against men; for you neither go in yourselves, nor do you allow those who are entering to go in."

It is instructive that Jesus used the precise words of Isaiah, their great prophet, to describe their hypocrisy. Notice His quote from Isaiah 29:13:

Mark 7:5-7 "He answered and said to them, "Well did Isaiah prophesy of you hypocrites, as it is written: 'This people honours Me with their lips, but their heart is far from Me. And in vain they worship Me, teaching as doctrines the commandments of men.'"

Jesus even accused them of being whitewashed tombs, disguising their inner corruption:

Matt 23:27-29 "Woe to you, scribes and Pharisees, hypocrites! For you are like whitewashed tombs which indeed appear beautiful outwardly, but inside are full of dead men's bones and all uncleanness. Even so you also outwardly appear righteous to men, but inside you are full of hypocrisy and lawlessness".

No wonder they wanted to kill Him! Outward self righteousness is the inevitable product of Pharisaic legalism. Jesus revealed their true motives: *Matt 23:5 "But all their works they do to be seen by men."* They were so filled with pride that they could not see that they would not practise what they had preached. In fact this was exactly what Jesus meant when He said *"for they say, and do not do"* (Matthew 23:3). It is important to note carefully however that (a) not all Pharisees were bad and (b) it is true to say that theologically the Lord Jesus was in many ways closest to the Pharisees! Jesus objected to the sheer hypocrisy: they were teaching man-made traditions but failing truly to keep the Law themselves.

Coming back to the Hebrew Roots Movement and those of like-minded persuasion, we need to tread carefully. The reference to "roots" is quite simply a (correct) allusion to Romans 11:18. It is the Hebraic root that supports the mainly Gentile church, not vice versa. However we need to note several things: (1) the root is singular – it is not plural! This might sound like a very minor, even fastidious objection, but we are not grafted in to a series of roots growing in all sorts of directions and perhaps emerging in all sorts of unlikely places! The root (singular) into which we are grafted is the olive root – and the olive tree is a symbol of Israel. Yet the so-called Hebrew Roots Movement can claim many and varied things. Some who claim to be a part of this "movement" (although whether they truly are, or whether they simply harbour an agenda is another matter!) seem to err towards the idea that all disciples of Jesus, whether Jewish or non-Jewish, are to be bound by the entire Mosaic "Law" as set out in the Old Testament. In this they appear to ignore totally the apostle Paul's clear instructions in Galatians chapter 5 where he is crystal clear that believers in Jesus are not to come "back" under the yoke of slavery – i.e. the Law. Indeed, the whole epistle to the Galatians majors on this key theme, as some Jewish believers were telling new converts from a Gentile/pagan background that they had to convert to Judaism before they could be true disciples of Jesus, and Paul was opposing them forcefully.

Some in the modern Jewish Roots Movement, it must be said, ignore the letter to the Galatians. However at the opposite extreme are those Christians who hold what must be described as "judeo-phobic" views – and I choose my words very deliberately. A 'phobia' is an unwarranted fear, so judeo-phobic is a perfectly legitimate description of this current within some Christian thinking. These Christians would rather that Romans chapter 11 was not in our Bibles, and so seek to reinterpret it – or worse still to ignore it completely! They also feel deeply uncomfortable that Jesus was (is) a Jew and that the name by which His mother Miriam called Him was Yeshua (or Y'shua) – actually Joshua in English! He never heard the English word "Jesus", which is an English translation of a Latin Translation of a Greek translation of His Hebrew name! True disciples of Jesus have to be simultaneously Galatians 5 people *and* Romans 11 people, holding these two currents within the Scriptures in holy and joyful tension with each other. In truth, it is not too difficult!

When people who call themselves "Christians" say that we *must* observe certain practices in order to secure our salvation (they would say to work out our salvation) then they are placing a burden on our necks that we are not required to carry. Indeed, Jesus Himself said **"my yoke is easy and my burden is light"** (Matthew 11:30). The context in which He said this was as He sought to bring comfort to all those who are "wearied" with rules and regulations. Immediately after saying this and in chapter 12 we come to the controversy concerning Jesus as the Lord of the Sabbath. We can say that the religious establishment were seeking to impose burdensome religious regulations on people, and from these burdens Jesus promised to relieve them; His simple call was "come and follow me" – and His call is the same today. None of this is to suggest that Yeshua in any way despised the Torah, but rather that the people generally needed relief from both the full Mosaic law (which was in a very real sense on its way out, in any case)[1] and especially from the oral law or the "second law" which reinforced and ring-fenced the biblical laws.

Some well-meaning people do indeed hint, suggest and sometimes even demand that we are obliged to maintain the full Law as we follow Jesus. They will often say that this performance does not lead to or threaten salvation, and yet they behave as though it does, sometimes (and in extreme cases) even breaking fellowship with those who deny this.

The fourteenth chapter of Paul's letter to the Roman church addresses this question. It will be worth readers pausing here to read the whole chapter. In it, Paul commands that we do not "judge" each other on the basis of, specifically, what we eat or the observance of certain "days".

He says that **"One person thinks that a certain day is more important than other days, whilst someone else thinks that all days are the same"** (Romans 14:5). So Paul is giving to the church absolute freedom in this matter, and although the letter does not specify, I would hazard a guess that Paul had in mind the Moedim. There would in any case have been severe, and probably insurmountable, practical difficulties for non-Jews living beyond the lands of Judea and Galilee in observing such Levitical rules; doubly so as many would have been slaves within the Roman Empire. How on earth could they have complied, except perhaps in mind and in spirit?

And yet.... There is another dimension to this. As we saw in chapter 3, the institutional church has taken upon itself the 'authority' to invent a liturgical year and associated celebrations and saints' days. Nowhere is this authority given, scripturally speaking. As we saw earlier, it is arguable that these "celebrations" and "saints' days" really obscure the clear gospel message contained in the Moedim, and are evidence of a very real effort to de-judaize the church and to separate the church from its root – this is known today as "replacement theology" and this obscuritanist teaching has many guises within the institutional church, both excusing and reinforcing the very real anti-Semitism within this church, that has existed like a semi dormant virus since the earliest post-apostolic times. Again I choose my words carefully and deliberately. I recognise they will offend some.

In my book *Rebel Church* I posited the view that soon – and I say specifically in the years 2017–2027 – many ordinary Christians are going to find it impossible to remain within *institutional churches* that
* follow the world's way in terms of the so-called equalities agenda;
* move towards thoroughgoing syncretism (that is, melding with other religions);
* preach what has to be described as a false gospel.

In this situation many will find themselves "frozen out" if not actively thrown out of many such *institutional churches* as their hierarchies refuse to tolerate dissent. Such Christians will be held up as old-fashioned, fundamentalist, intolerant and extreme. As these Christians find new homes, two vital questions are likely to manifest themselves:
1. If we are no longer welcome to worship on Sundays, then why not meet for corporate worship on Saturdays, which remains the day on which the Lord would have attended His synagogue? This has nothing to do with spiritual "performance" or of "salvation"; rather, it is one of practicalities. The real and progressively pressing question remains "why not?" It would honour Jesus by honouring our root, into which we are in-grafted. Indeed, as we worship Jesus in times that we may come to recognise very much as *the latter days*, will this become a distinctive, marking us out as Jesus' people, as opposed to all those who, in the words of Paul to Timothy, have "**a form of godliness, but denying its**

power" (2 Timothy 3:5). Note carefully the uncomfortable words of Paul about avoiding such people.

2. Why not structure our worshipful year around the Moedim? As this book has shown, each "holy convocation" speaks about the life, death, mission, ministry and second coming of Jesus, not to mention His eternal "tabernacling" with His people. Could it be that this modern rediscovery of our root – and especially of the Moedim, is a gift from Jesus to prepare His people for His second coming?

I cannot offer a definitive answer for you in your personal situation. Speaking for myself and for other believers known to me, we are beginning to explore the practicalities of marking the Moedim. I cannot foresee this ever becoming a "heavy duty". Jesus' yoke is easy and His burden is light! There would be little sense or attraction in building a sukkot in a northern climate, nor in crime-ridden areas! But to mark these celebrations, in some way, through focus on them, at a spiritual level, seems entirely level-headed and sensible. Why not?

A wise retired vicar once commented to me that "we do not correct 2000 years of false Christian praxis by adopting 2000 years of false Jewish praxis"! This was in the context of his having reviewed a book manuscript which was very much in favour of adopting a Hebrew calendar. My reviewer, who remains very much well disposed to things Hebraic, was surely correct and we declined to publish the book, as its writer was certainly of the view that his Hebraic worship pattern *must* be adopted and that failure to do so is an active defiance of the Lord. It is notable that people who hold such theological views can be persuasive and sometimes can support their views with scripture – but such scriptures are usually taken out of their full context and are, to that extent, misleading. Some who urge the adoption of Hebrew practices seem blissfully unaware that much of what is Jewish cultural observance has nothing to do with Scripture. We should note clearly that Rosh Hashannah, Purim, Tish B'Av and Chanukah all fall into this category. We may learn useful things about Israel, its people, its culture and its religion from these practices, but crucially they say nothing of Jesus – and even the obscure Rabbinic remembrance of the Moedim has become polluted by non-commanded elements, or even pagan elements, as we saw in Part 2 of this book.

The Gospel in the Moedim

The Moedim are very much the gospel and the theological history – and future – of mankind acted out in seven celebrations. It is a wonderful truth that we can structure the full gospel message around these seven events. Let us do so here:

Passover

For all alike have sinned and fallen short of the Glory of God (Romans 3:23). We all know that we are not the people that we would like to be, let alone the people that a Holy and Righteous God expects us to be. We are sinners in need of salvation. Not one of us would like to have even our thought life exposed to public scrutiny, let alone things we have said or done. In our more honest moments we acknowledge our need of cleansing – of our need for someone to save us from ourselves. God always had in mind a plan to rescue human beings from the grip of sin, but He was never going to force His solution on us. We have to receive His solution as a gift.

And what is this solution? God prefigured it through Passover, when literally the penalty for our sins passes over us, the guilty ones, and is laid to the account of the Lord Jesus. He has given His life for sinners who do not deserve Him. It is a true reflection of God's love for all humans that He does not leave us without the prospect of salvation. How does God love the world? **"For God thus loved the world"** wrote the apostle John **"that He gave His only Son, that whoever believes on Him shall not die but shall have eternal life"** (John 3:16). The "thus" in the foregoing reflects verse 14 – so *how* did God love the world? He loved it by lifting up His Son – on the cross of crucifixion. In His death is our healing.

Unleavened Bread

Jesus was killed, there is no doubt about that – the Romans knew all about killing people. Jesus did not swoon and later revive. He was dead and buried! Yet He was without sin. The "leaven" of sin was not in Him, and so death could not hold Him. The same applies to us – as we appropriate Jesus' victory over death, and His defeating death and leading death as a captive (Ephesians 4:7-9). Death is defeated and need never again hold any fear for us!

First Fruits

Jesus demonstrated His victory over death in his resurrection. Death is the only real weapon that the devil has over us, and now Jesus has defeated it. The devil loves death. Jesus loves life! Men have sought to disprove the resurrection of Jesus from the very beginning – their attempts have failed and serve only to demonstrate their anger at the empty grave. All their efforts are for nothing; Jesus lives and He is coming back, not as the suffering servant of Isaiah 53, but as the ruler of the world. Jesus is the "first fruit" of a vast harvest – of all those that place their faith and trust in Him, becoming His disciples, with all that this wonderful status implies.

Latter First Fruits

There is a time for sowing and reaping in this world. The good news of Jesus is a message that is like good seed. It sometimes falls on stony ground, into the minds of those that are closed to Jesus. But often it falls into good soil, into the hearts and minds of those who will listen to this good news of sins forgiven and new (and eternal) life in Jesus. During the hot summer months the harvest is gathered, and the 2,000 years since Jesus' ascension have been a gathering period. All those who come to Jesus in faith and repentance will be saved – for all who call on the name of the Lord will be saved (see Joel 2:32, Acts 2:21; Romans 10:13). This is a guarantee!

What is the name into which we are to believe? What is the name we are to call out to? It is the name Yeshua (Jesus) which means Saviour. We can have absolute assurance of Jesus' power and will to save:

Jesus said it:
Luke 18:17 – accept like a child
– there is nothing deeply intellectual about this!
John 4:14 – whoever drinks will never thirst;
John 3:1-21 – the need to be born again;
John 17:3 – this is eternal life, to know God and to know
Jesus, Whom He sent.

The Bible affirms it:

Ephesians 1:4-7 – we have redemption through His blood;

1 John 2:2 – He is the atoning sacrifice;

1 John 5:11-13 – life is in His Son;

1 Peter3:18 – Christ died once for all;

Romans 3:21-25 – we gain righteousness through faith;

Romans 4:25 – **because of our sins He was handed over to die, and He was raised to life in order to put us right with God**. (Good News)

Romans 8:38-39 – He will never leave you;

Romans 10:9 – if you confess, you will be saved.

All of history points towards it:

Ephesians 1:9 – when the times had reached their fulfilment;

John 1:1 and 12 – in the beginning .... we have the right to become children of God;

Exodus 14 – the crossing of the Red Sea is a picture of baptism – of crossing from death to life;

Isaiah 53 and Psalm 22 – the suffering servant and the crucifixion is prefigured;

Jeremiah 31:31 – a new covenant is promised. And in Isaiah 42:6 this new covenant is enlarged to cover all mankind.

Today we live very much in the Latter First Fruits period of mankind's history. But this period of grace will ultimately come to an end, when Jesus returns. In the meantime, Jesus has given a very clear command and mandate to preach and take the gospel to all peoples everywhere on earth, making them His disciples, baptising them in the name of the Father and of the Son and of the Holy Spirit; and teaching them to obey everything He has commanded. (Matthew 28:20).

Trumpets

Jesus' return is prefigured in Scripture. It seems that in some way the future global reign of Messiah will be announced with a trumpet call (Revelation 11:15-17; 1 Thessalonians 4:16). No one on earth will be unaware of this happening!

Atonement

We can look forward to that triumphant return and to the future, whether or not we live to see it – many of us will be "called home" first. We look forward with confidence to the future because we know our sins have been atoned for, the debt has been paid and the Lord Jesus is the One Who has paid that debt. Our task is to follow Him, seeking His Holy Spirit to enable us and to empower us.

Atonement also reminds us that there is a judgement to follow. In that sense the good news is not all good news! But perhaps it *is* in reality truly good news that there will be a judgement and that all the wicked rebellions against God, and all the evil things that have ever been done down through history will ultimately and permanently be punished. That is dreadfully sad for those who must face this eternal punishment, yet it demonstrates the righteousness and holiness of God. He will never "tip the wink" at sin – sin is serious. If it was not, then surely God would have found a less costly way of dealing with it, than the way He chose – involving the crucifixion of His own dear Son.

Tabernacles

Tabernacles reminds us of the latter times of trouble in this life, and of Israel's wilderness experience. It reminds us that we are a pilgrim people on our journey to the Promised Land of our heavenly home. Our life as "witnesses" here can sometimes also be a wilderness experience. Jesus was quite clear that in this life we will face opposition if we are His disciples. He said **"know that if the world hates you that it hated me first"** (John 15:18). This is true both at as practical level and at a spiritual level – the world hates Jesus because it does not want to surrender its sins. Rather than recognise Jesus as truly God and welcome God's right to rule in our hearts, accepting His gracious remedy of salvation, people would rather be their own "god". And for just a short time they can, in a very limited sense, be their own "demi-god" in their own tiny space. But in this they will find no true happiness and no true peace, only the nagging doubt that there is a future – a "one day" – that they must sooner or later face. Then there will be consequences....

But Jesus will certainly "tabernacle" with His *chosen people* from every nation, tribe and tongue. We will have wonderful, true and permanent fellowship with our Lord! Jesus calls us His friends (John 15:15) and in a very real sense that is how we know Him. Not in any over-familiar sense, but in the sure knowledge that He knows us individually, He cares for us individually, He certainly loves us, and has "prepared a place" for us – especially for you and for me. **"In my Father's house there are many rooms"** (John 14:2), and, **"I am going to prepare a place for you"**. What a wonderful prospect, to tabernacle with our loving Lord through all eternity.

So the seven Moedim, those appointed times, those appointed meetings, are in truth very precise types and shadows of the salvation plan of God. The God Who truly loves – not in some cheap or shallow "sentimental love" in the world's way of understanding, and not because of any innate goodness in us. It is a love that has demonstrated itself in the most public and profound way. The true love of God is the *hesed* of the Old Testament and the *agape* of the New – a love which costs and a love which hurts.

This is love. Not that we loved God, but that he loved us and sent his Son as an atoning sacrifice for our sins (1 John 4:10).

Note that in this context the word is "loved" – and we see that it is very specifically about the *single event* of the sacrifice of Jesus. Jesus prayed not to a "loving Father" as so many of us presume to do (in fact this term is not found in the Bible at all). No, Jesus prayed to His *Righteous Father* (John 17:25).

Whether we are Jewish or Gentile, each one of us needs to really know personally, at the deepest level, certain great truths about God which are revealed throughout the Bible. Some of these have been touched on elsewhere, but now we draw together some essential threads. There are three wonderful truths about God that we should not lose sight of: His righteousness, His justice and His mercy.

We can say with assurance that God is absolutely *righteous*, perfect and just. He is our Creator and He does not owe us anything at all. He is the Giver of all good things. Everything He does for us flows from His grace – meaning that *every* good gift is freely given and completely undeserved. Scripture also teaches consistently that He is *merciful*. We should never imagine that this means He can merely wink at and tolerate sin. His righteousness and justice would not be consistent with that. God has revealed to us that His righteousness entails punishment of all sin (either in this world or the next) – and He has made very clear in His written Word what is meant by that. His justice is perfect, which in itself should cause each one of us to tremble. Human rebellion, flowing from the Fall, is and has been evident in every society and every individual – with the sole exception of Yeshua (Jesus), the Messiah.

We should be crystal clear that God's mercy does not confer any "rights" on us – *we are always absolutely dependent on His mercy*, and again we see at so many places in the Bible that this means our attitude should be one of *humility*. Yeshua commended a humble and penitent attitude in people, and His apostles did likewise. In our "pattern" prayer that we call The Lord's Prayer He showed us we need constantly to be thankful and seek forgiveness for any way in which we have offended God – and always to be ready and willing to forgive others.

In His mercy, God opened the Way of salvation to us. *He didn't have to do so*. It was all of grace (free gift) that God the Father gave His only-begotten Son Yeshua to die the death that our sins deserved – *for us*. As we have seen, that involved undeserved suffering – Jesus is our Passover Lamb. It involved the shedding of blood as the just requirements of the Law were perfectly met. In the Passion and crucifixion of the Messiah we see that *the righteous requirements of the Law were met* on behalf of all who would believe (and go on believing) in Yeshua. The penalty of sin was thereby paid in full, the wrath of God against sin was satisfied, and in that divine act we have seen the singular *agape love* of God. It was a one-time event which had been foreshadowed and prophesied in various ways to which Scripture testifies.

The Bible speaks of this special kind of love using the Greek word agape, which means in this context that something has been given or done for the undeserving person – something that is *needed* that he or she could not do for him/herself. Without that *singular historical event* of the saving death of Jesus, followed by His burial and resurrection from the dead, we would be without hope. Thus God provided what we need to *begin* the Christian life, all of which is given to us personally. What we need, and by grace can have, is:

* repentance toward God;
* believing in Yeshua (Jesus);
* baptism into His name in water; and
* baptism in Holy Spirit.

Moreover, He has provided everything we need to *continue* in the Christian "walk" of obedience and trust, in which we have all the help, resources and guidance we need from the same indwelling Holy Spirit as we *go on being filled* with the Spirit and growing in the Word. So it is that to begin on this divinely offered Way of Salvation; we have to let God do something for us – which goes right against the grain of our inevitable and spurious sense of independence and self-sufficiency. Praise Him for this wonderful provision!

Note

[1] The Second Temple system was in its last few decades by this time. Jesus knew that the Second Temple would be destroyed – and so it was in AD70. Levitical ritual would very soon become a thing of the past.

APPENDICES

APPENDIX 1

HOW THE MOEDIM ARE PROGRESSIVELY

Passover –   a permanent commemoration

    –   instruction given before the event of
         the striking-down of the first-born
         of Egypt

}   EXODUS 12

The Biblical Feasts (the appointed meetings
– or Moedim)

1   –   Passover

2   –   Unleavened Bread

3   –   First Fruits

4   –   Latter First Fruits ("feast of weeks", "Shavuot")

5   –   Trumpets

6   –   Atonement

7   –   Tabernacles

}   LEVITICUS 23
     = complete

The context of these God-given instructions is important:

Exodus 12 is given in the immediate (12 hours?) events prior to the striking down of Egypt's first born and the associated passing over of those who are marked with the sign of blood.

Leviticus 23 – the whole book regulates the spiritual life of first and second Temple Israel. In chapter 22 we find rules for priests. Chapter 23 gives us rules for the worshipful year, starting with Sabbath (Shabbat) and then moving directly to the seven Moedim.

Deuteronomy 16 – found in the context of instructions from Moses to the people of Israel. It is interesting that Moses should concentrate on just four of the seven Moedim; the words of Moses in the entire book are focused on the building of a redeemed (set apart) people. Whilst today the detailed Levitical rules no longer apply yet they teach us much about the need for holiness, and of the true nature of a holy redeeming God. In

UNVEILED IN OUR MODERN BIBLES

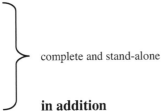

complete and stand-alone

in addition

NUMBERS 28:16–31 and 29:1–40
This adds detail to the Temple ritual.
It has no direct bearing on believers today.

DEUTERONOMY 16:1–16
This adds detail of the "how" of:

- Passover
- First Fruits
- Latter First Fruits
- Tabernacles

arguably the four Moedim that are of most relevance to the entire world throughout all time

Passover = separation from sin
First Fruits = resurrection
Latter First Fruits = global harvest
Tabernacles = eternal joy, eternal home

---

this context, the focus by Moses on the four of the seven Moedim that are of most immediate day to day concern to *all* people(s) at *all* times, must be of special joy to the true disciple of the Lord Jesus.

The book of Numbers is the account of Israel's wanderings during the forty years from the time they left Mount Sinai until they reached the eastern border of the Promised Land. Numbers 28 and 29 recount events when the Israelites dwelt in Moab and provides more depth to the Moedim associated with Tabernacle worship.

APPENDIX 2

DIFFERENT NAMES FOR BIBLICAL FEASTS

There are multiple names used to describe these feasts. Some are functional, others are cultural and/or traditional. Throughout this book we have generally used the functional name in English. However readers will from time to time come across other names – and this can be downright confusing. It is hoped that this chart will bring some clarity.

Names of the Hebrew Moedim

COMMON ENGLISH	HEBREW	ALT. HEBREW	ALT. "CHRISTIAN"
Passover	Pesach	–	"Good Friday"
Unleavened Bread	Hag HaMatzot	–	"Easter Eve"
First Fruits	Ha Bikkorim	Sfirat HaOmer	"Easter"
Latter First Fruits	Shavuot	Feast of Weeks	Pentecost
Trumpets	Yom Teruah	Rosh Hashanah	–
Atonement	Yom Kippur	–	–
Tabernacles	Sukkot	Booths	Tabernacles

Note that in regard to Trumpets and Rosh Hashanah, the latter is the de facto replacement for Trumpets and today marks the Jewish New Year. As such it is not in accordance with the objective of the Moed of Trumpets, which has now largely been forgotten by Rabbinic Judaism. Rosh Hashanah is not a Moed.

APPENDIX 3

A Covenant God

God is a promise-keeping God. He makes His covenants and we must respond to those covenants, either in faith or rejection.

Which covenants are still in force? The table on the next two pages suggests it is only the Moses covenant that has been replaced – and that it has been replaced by the Messianic covenant, which ushers in a new age.

Each covenant has been given a number for ease of reference. Each row in the table shows with whom the covenant was established, and its conditionality.

Note to Appendix 3

Does this matter? Is this just ancient history or dry theology? Many Christians hold that these truths speak into our situation today; in particular into the world in which we currently live, the growth of the Messianic Jewish movement and the restoration of the Jewish people to their biblical home land. Are these accidents of history, or is God working out his covenantal promises as He said He would? Finally, these texts help us to understand which covenants are timeless and therefore still apply. Crucially they suggest that it is the Moses covenant that has been 'replaced', by being extended and enlarged to cover all mankind. Today God appoints a royal priesthood of all those who are true disciples of Jesus.

	Made with	Key text	Commentary
0	Adam	Gen 2:16	We are free to live in peace and to enjoy all that God gives. We are not, however, free to sin without consequence. Whilst this is not truly a covenant, it is included in this list to give perspective to the other five covenants.
1	Noah	Gen 9:16	God in fact made an extended covenant with Noah, in terms of protecting Noah and his family. Gen 6:18; Gen 8:21b; Gen 9:3 (reminiscent of Gen 1:29); Gen 9:11 through 17.
2	Abraham	Gen 12:2-3	Repeated and emphasised: Gen 12:7; Gen 15:5-7; Gen 22:16-18; Ex 3:8, Ex 3:17; Ex 6:6-8
3	Moses	Ex 19:5-6	The Hebrews become a nation of priests: this is a blessing to the whole world. Ex 20 (all) and Ex 34:10ff set out the conditions applicable.
4	David	2 Sam 7:13-16	God promises to establish a house for Himself forever (2 Sam 7:13). This is a direct Messianic promise, as God works out His purpose to bless all Mankind. See 1 Sam 16:13. Also 2 Sam 7 (all) and 2 Sam 23:5.
5	Messianic		Having established His covenant with Israel through Abraham and promised a House through David, the covenantal promises now become more explicit, as God points towards what the Messianic office entails, how the Messianic line would bring life from death, and Who that Messiah would be - principally in terms of the suffering servant. God reveals these truths through three major prophets:
5A	Jeremiah (what)	Jer 24:7; Jer 31:31-40	The promise of a new covenant becomes explicit. Jeremiah chapter 33 (all) links the promise of restoration with the Land and through the line of David. It foretells both the Messiah and a future age of peace and righteousness yet to be seen.
5B	Ezekiel (how)	Ezek 37 (all)	Ezekiel 37 shows how God will bring life from death. The restoration of the Jewish Nation, and through them, the provision of the Messiah of the whole world.
5C	Isaiah (who)	Is 52:13 -53:12	The suffering servant becomes explicit: Is 8:14; 9:1-7; 11:1-5; 32:1-4; 50:2-8; and Is 52:13-53:12; and Is 54 through to 56:8

	Made with	Applies to	Conditionality
0	Adam	Through Adam, applies to all mankind	The conditionality is only spelled out in God's gracious refusal to allow mankind to eat from the tree of life (Gen 3:22)
1	Noah	All mankind	Unconditional
2	Abraham	Through the Hebrews, applies to all mankind	Unconditional
3	Moses	The Hebrews	Conditional on obedience
4	David	David	Unconditional
5	Messianic		
5A	Jeremiah (what)	Through the Hebrews, applies to all mankind	Conditional on obedience
5B	Ezekiel (how)	Through the Hebrews, applies to all mankind	Conditional on obedience
5C	Isaiah (who)	Through the Hebrews, applies to all mankind	Conditional on obedience

APPENDIX 4

THE MAGNIFICENT SEVEN

The number seven recurs throughout scripture. Whilst we should avoid anything like numerology (the study of numbers and mathematics in the belief that they reveal secret and esoteric messages) we cannot avoid noticing that certain numbers are repeated throughout scripture. These numbers have an undoubted special significance:

Twelve

This is always a reference in some way to Israel. We note that the Lord Jesus chose twelve apostles, being somehow the inaugurators of a new, *enlarged Israel* comprised of all those who place their trust and faith in Jesus the Messiah and live as His disciples (with all that this implies!), whether they are Jews or non-Jews. Israel itself consisted of twelve tribes. Jerusalem had twelve gates, and this is replicated in the New Jerusalem which will be given by God in the future (Revelation 21:21). In the book of Revelation there are 144,000 Jewish people "marked" with God's seal on the foreheads – that is $12 \times 12 = 144$. We might say it is Israel x Israel. We should note in this passage from Revelation we find that the 144,000 of Revelation 7:4 is immediately followed by a statement that there was an enormous crowd that "no one could number", from every race, tribe, language and nation. It seems in some mysterious way, that Israel is the opening point, or even the "gate" through which all of human-kind encounter the risen Lord Jesus. We only need to reflect that Jesus is David's son, and so Israel's eternal king, to see the reality that, in some way, Israel as God's chosen people provides the instrument of reconciliation of all peoples to God the Father, through God the Son. Never forgetting, of course, that Jesus described Himself as "the Gate" (John 10:9) as well as His Father as the gate-keeper (John 10:3).

Whether the fact that there are twelve months in the year is also in some way to encourage us to reflect upon Israel is a question to which there is no definitive answer. Should we be reflecting on God's gracious mercies in and through this *chosen people* month by month?

Three

This number seems to be always reflective of the relationship of what Christians rightly call The Holy Trinity, that wonderful if mysterious relationship of God the Father, with God the Son and God the Holy Spirit. Three also seems to be a reflection of completeness, though not to the same extent as the number seven. There were three righteous Patriarchs before the flood (Abel, Enoch and Noah). After the flood the great Patriarchs of Israel were Abraham, Isaac and Jacob – who was later, of course, re-named Israel. It is correctly pointed out that there are 27 books in the New Testament (3x3x3). Could this be a reflection of God's perfect (and complete) revelation of the outworking of the new covenant, centred on the redemptive work of the Father, Son and Holy Spirit? In this redemption, there is completion; in other words there is nothing more to be added, nothing more to be said, and nothing more to be done.

We note also that Jesus prayed three times in the Garden of Gethsemane before His arrest. He was placed on the cross at the 3rd hour of the day (9 a.m.) and died at the 9th hour (3 p.m.). There were 3 hours of darkness that covered the land while Jesus was suffering on the cross from the 6th hour to the 9th hour. Three is the number of resurrection. Christ was dead for three days and three nights, before being resurrected.

Apart from the number seven, three is the most common number in the book of Revelation. An angel cries out three woes to the people who live on earth, alerting them to more trials yet to come (Revelation 8:13 and 9:12). The murdered bodies of the Two Witnesses will not be allowed to be buried but rather will lie openly in Jerusalem for three (and a half) days before they are resurrected. Three unclean spirits will be allowed to deceive the whole world to fight against the returning Messiah Jesus in what is called the battle of Armageddon (Revelation 16:13-16). The New Jerusalem, created by God and installed on the new earth, will be shaped like a square with three gates on each side (Revelation 21:13). God Himself is described, in the very beginning of the book of Revelation, as a Being "which is, and which was, and which is to come" (Revelation 1:4).

As we have seen throughout this book, there are three clear phases (or periods) during which the biblical Moedim are effective: these are the spring feasts (Passover, Unleavened Bread and First fruits) the beginning of the summer harvest (Latter First Fruits) and the three autumn festivals (Trumpets, Atonement and Tabernacles).

The numbers three and seven interestingly coalesce in the book of Daniel. In the second chapter, King Nebuchadnezzar had a dream of a giant statue whose head was of gold, arms and chest of silver, belly and hips of brass, legs of iron, and feet of a mixture of iron and clay (Daniel 2:31-33). Daniel told him that he, Nebuchadnezzar, was the head of gold (vs 37-38) and went on to explain the significance of the other elements of the dream. Whether Daniel's explanation went, proverbially, 'straight to the head' of King Nebuchadnezzar is perhaps not for us to say, but in the next chapter Nebuchadnezzar made an image of gold to be worshipped. Nebuchadnezzar called together seven kinds of officials to the dedication of the image: (1) princes, (2) governors, (3) captains, (4) judges, (5) treasurers (6) counsellors, (7) sheriffs. The penalty for refusing to worship the image was death by being cast into a burning fiery furnace. Three Hebrew men refused to worship the image and were cast into that furnace of death, yet were brought out alive, surely an oblique picture of the resurrection, and signified by the number three; three were thrown in and three were brought out alive. The furnace had been heated seven times hotter than it had ever been before! Here we see a complete and definitive deliverance for God's faithful people from the power of death (Daniel 3:1-27). When those three true Israelites emerged from the furnace of death, there was not a trace of fire upon their bodies or their clothing. It is rightly observed that when Christ brings His people out of death there will not be a trace of death left on them. They will be completely and definitively delivered from its power.

Numerology – a simple warning
Whilst these usages of numbers within the Bible are too numerous and at too many clearly *strategic revelatory points* for us to ignore, and are clearly there for a purpose, we must not allow fascination with them to become some spurious "theology" in its own right. There have always been false teachers who seek to make themselves look significant (in their own eyes and in the eyes of those eager to be led) with their "hidden" or esoteric mysteries, which, surprise, surprise (!) only they know about

– but which they are prepared to share with you if (a) you will follow them and (b) you will give them some money! We are told to fix our eyes upon Jesus, the author and finisher of our faith (Hebrews 12:2). If nothing else, it is hoped that this book with its focus on the connection of the Moedim to the life, death, resurrection, mission and ministry of the Lord Jesus, has not fallen into this trap, but rather, has helped to reflect the sheer majesty of His achievements.

Seven

The number seven is always, in the Bible, a number of completeness, of divine perfection or something that is completely finished, as in the creation "week" of Genesis 1:1 to 2:3. God might have chosen to create the earth in a single "day" or over multiple years. However, He chose to invest six days in creating the earth, and then rested on the seventh. In doing this he was clearly providing for mankind a pattern to be followed. God "rested" on the seventh day, not because He was tired but as an example for us to follow. We are commanded to work six days and to rest on the seventh. This is the fourth of the ten commandments of Exodus chapter 20. It is repeated in Exodus 34:21 "Six days you shall work, but on the seventh day you shall rest. In ploughing time and in harvest you shall rest." In the Ten Commandments the first three commandments are about God Himself (we are back to the number three!) but the fourth is about Sabbath (Shabbat). The weekly rest is a pattern for us to follow and by which to be blessed. Disregard your weekly rest too often and you will quickly notice the practical implications!

There are numerous references to, or uses of, the number seven in the Bible. For examples:

- No animal could be sacrificed until it was seven days old (Exodus 22:30).
- The Lord would discipline Israel up to sevenfold (up to seven times) if they refused to obey Him (Leviticus 26:18).
- Jesus condemns the religious leaders (teachers of the law and Pharisees) seven times in Matthew 23.
- Jesus uses seven parables in Matthew chapter 13.
- There are seven letters to the seven churches in the book of Revelation (chapters 2 and 3).

- There are seven trumpets announcing judgments by God in the book of Revelation (chapter 8).
- Joshua and Israel marched around Jericho seven times while seven priests blew seven trumpets before the walls came crashing down (Joshua 6:3-4).
- Elisha told the military commander Naaman to bathe in the Jordan River seven times and he would be healed of his leprosy (2 Kings 5:10).
- There are seven qualities or attributes of the Messiah cited in Isaiah 11:2-5.
- There are seven things that the Lord hates cited in Proverbs 6:16.
- There were seven stems to the lampstand in Israel's tabernacle (Exodus 25:37).
- There were seven angels pouring out seven bowls of the wrath of God in the Book of Revelation (16:1).

Hopefully by now we should be seeing the pattern and its importance: wherever something is mentioned seven times the Lord is making an emphatic statement and one not to be ignored. It is as if God is saying "I am making this *perfectly* clear to you, so take notice". The number seven is also the number of perfection.

Additional information on the Biblical meaning of the number 7

Jesus performed *seven miracles* on God's holy Sabbath Day (which ran from Friday sunset to Saturday sunset), thus affirming its continued sacredness to God and necessity in the life of the believer:

1. Jesus healed the withered hand of a man attending synagogue (Matthew 12:9).
2. At a Capernaum synagogue he cast out an unclean spirit that possessed a man (Mark 1:21).
3. Immediately after the above miracle, Jesus healed Peter's wife's mother (Mark 1:29).
4. A woman attending synagogue, who had been made sick by a demon for eighteen years, was released from her bondage (Luke 13:11).
5. At a Pharisee's house eating a meal with the host and several teachers of the Law, Jesus healed a man with dropsy (Luke 14:2).

6. A man who was disabled and unable to walk was healed at the pool of Bethesda (John 5:8-9)
7. Jesus healed a man born blind at the *pool of Siloam* (John 9:14)

Are these seven Sabbath healings merely a numerical coincidence, or is Jesus telling us that He is the Lord of the Sabbath?

Interestingly, mankind was created on the sixth day of creation. In some passages of the Bible, the number six is associated with mankind. In Revelation "the number of the beast" is called "the number of a man. That number is 666 (Revelation 13:18). If God's number is 7, then man's is 6. Six always falls short of seven, as we are obliquely reminded that **"all have sinned and fall short of the glory of God"** (Romans 3:23). Man is not God, just as 6 is not 7!

Multiples of 7 also figure in the biblical narrative: the "seventy weeks" prophecy in Daniel 9:24 concerns 490 years (7 times 7 times 10). Jeremiah 29:10 predicted the Babylonian Captivity would last for seventy years (7 times 10). According to Leviticus 25:8, the Year of Jubilee was to begin after the passing of every forty-ninth year (7 times 7) leading to a "new start" – almost a new life – for all those benefitting from the Jubilee year. Jesus told Peter to forgive a wrongdoer "seventy times seven" times (Matthew 18:22) – in other words, *completely*. There are passages in which the number seven is associated with God's judgment: the seven bowls of the Great Tribulation, for example (Revelation 16:1), or God's warning to Israel in Leviticus 26:18.

The total number of times the number seven is used in the Bible is more than seven hundred. If we also count the words related to *seven* (terms like *sevenfold* or *seventy* or *seven hundred*), the count is still higher. **We must note carefully however** that not every instance of the number 7 in the Bible carries a deeper significance: sometimes, a 7 is just a 7. We must be cautious about attaching symbolic meanings to any and every text, especially when Scripture is not explicit about such meanings. However, there are numerous instances when God is surely communicating the idea of divine completeness, perfection and wholeness by means of the number seven.

Your author has occasionally heard the odd sermon given, at a church building on a Sunday, where the speaker links numbers rather randomly and makes profound-sounding assertions based on these linkages. It has to be said that such random *number crunching* is always dubious. They may impress some, but unless these numerical linkages are clearly of God, then they must be of man (or in the imagination of the sermon-giver!). It may also upset some readers to understand that the basis of all "dispensational" theology is dubious if not outright spurious. This line of teaching has it that there are seven periods in the history of humankind that are called "dispensations": Innocence, Conscience, Government, Patriarchal, Law, Grace, and the Millennial Age. Whilst it is easy to see how this sounds rather profound (and might in truth be a useful framework for thinking about God's dealings with mankind) *it is not something that is clearly taught in scripture*. Indeed this may be a precise example of random linkages that are not authorised by the Holy Spirit (the inspirer of all Scripture – 2 Timothy 3:16). Having said that, dispensational "theology" is not to be seen as wicked, but simply that it is misguided!

Final examples of the number seven in Scripture

The word *finished* is connected in the Bible with the number *seven*. In Revelation 10:7 we read, **"But in the days of the voice of the seventh angel, when he shall begin to sound, the mystery of God should be finished, as he hath declared..."** (KJV).

"It is *done*" is another expression found in connection with the number Seven: "And the *seventh* angel poured out his vial into the air; and there came a great voice out of the temple of heaven, from the throne saying, It is done." (Revelation 16:17).

Noah took the clean beasts into the ark by *sevens* (Genesis 7:2) *seven* days after Noah went into the ark the flood came (Genesis 7:10). Peter tells about the long-suffering of God waiting in the days of Noah (1 Peter 3:21). Those *seven* days *completed* God's time of waiting.

Before Aaron and his sons entered their priestly work they were consecrated during a period of *seven* days (Leviticus 8:31-36). Here we see a picture of a life *completely* or *wholly* consecrated or dedicated to the Lord for service.

On the Day of Atonement the high priest sprinkled the sacrificial blood upon the mercy seat *seven* times (Leviticus 16:14). This again is a picture of the *completeness* of the redemptive work of Messiah Jesus.

"By his own blood he entered in once into the holy place, having obtained eternal redemption for us" (Hebrews 9:12). When Messiah Jesus offered Himself that act *finished* or concluded the sacrificial offerings and its sacrificial system. They were ended. No longer must we place sacrifices upon an altar.

There were *seven* branches on the *candlestick* in the *Holy Place* in the Tabernacle. This illustrates the *complete* light of God for the souls of human beings.

Solomon was *seven* years in building the Temple and kept the Feast for *seven* days. Job had *seven* sons. When his friends came to visit him they sat *seven* days and *seven* nights in silence, and afterward they were required to offer a burnt offering of *seven* bullocks and *seven* rams. Naaman washed *seven* times in the Jordan. The Lord Jesus spoke *seven* words from the Cross. *Seven* men of honest report were chosen to administer the alms of the church in Acts 6:1-7. There were *seven* years of plenty and *seven* years of famine in Egypt during the days of Joseph.

Seven times in the Book of Revelation blessing of the Lord are promised to His people. These have been dubbed the "Beatitudes of Revelation". They are found in 1:3; 14:13; 16:15; 19:9; 20:6; 22:7, 22:14.

Seven times the Book of Life is mentioned in the Bible. As we have already seen the Book of Revelation is a Book of *sevens*. It highlights *seven* churches (surely representative of all types of church and their weaknesses, as well as their strengths), *seven* seals, *seven* trumpets, *seven* personages, *seven* veils, *seven* dooms, *seven* new things.

The Lord Jesus instructed us to "forgive *seventy* times *seven*". In other words, He is saying: keep on forgiving until you are complete; or even: forgive as I have forgiven you. Even the duration of Israel's great punishments for idolatry was based upon this law of *sevens*. Their captivity in Babylon was for *seventy* years, ten periods of *sevens* (Jeremiah 25:11-12; Daniel 19:2).

The Sabbath of Years
The Sabbath is not only a day, but also a year. In the same way that every seventh day is a Shabbat (Sabbath in Hebrew), so every seventh year is a Sabbath year, which is to be kept distinct and separate from the six preceding years.

The LORD said to Moses at Mount Sinai, "Speak to the Israelites and say to them: 'When you enter the land I am going to give you, the land itself must observe a Sabbath to the LORD. For six years sow your fields, and for six years prune your vineyards and gather their crops. But in the seventh year the land is to have a year of Sabbath rest, a Sabbath to the LORD. Do not sow your fields or prune your vineyards (Leviticus 25:1-4).

During this Sabbath year God commanded that no work would be done on the land. **"For six years you are to sow your fields and harvest the crops, but during the seventh year let the land lie unplowed and unused. Then the poor among your people may get food from it, and the wild animals may eat what is left. Do the same with your vineyard and your olive grove"** (Exodus 23:10-11). Precisely how this worked out in terms of the economics and practicalities of agricultural life is not clear to us. To prevent the Israelites from experiencing any shortages or other hardships during the Sabbath year, God promised that in the year immediately preceding the sabbatical period the land would yield fruit sufficient for the next three years (Leviticus 25:21). We can trust, then, that the God Who provided the rule, would also honour its observance. We can say that during this Sabbath year, not only would the people rest, but the land itself would rest. It has been suggested that the modern practice of periodically allowing a field to *lie fallow* for a year is an acknowledgement of the wisdom of God's command. Furthermore, during the Sabbath year the Israelites were to leave their fields, vineyards and olive groves open for the poor to glean.

On the last day of this Sabbath year (on Elul 29), Israelites were to be released from debts owed to other Israelites.

"At the end of every seven years you must cancel debts. This is how it is to be done: Every creditor shall cancel any loan they have made to a fellow Israelite. They shall not require payment from anyone among their own people, because the LORD's time for canceling debts has been proclaimed" (Deuteronomy 15:1-2).

Lack of space prevents us from exploring this fully, but we can assert that in this we see both God's wisdom and mercy at work: the financial transformation (or even "default/reset" to use a computing term) would rescue people from debts where they could not repay, and dissuade rampant money lenders from ruthlessly exploiting their economic and legal power over the poor. Every seventh year all debts were wiped away – in this we undoubtedly see a 'picture' or a 'type' of salvation through Messiah Jesus.

The original Hebrew language calls this release from debts a *shemitah*, and so this became known as the *shemitah year*. In recent years within the Christian church there has been a reawakening and a reassessment of the shemitah and what it means.[1] In biblical times, shemitah became the popular name of Elul 29, and each seventh year was known as the shemitah year. The shemitah is a different sort of Moed – that appointed time – where the year becomes a Sabbath rest (pointing to Jesus, our Sabbath rest). But the imagery of shemitah goes further still: every seventh shemitah leads into a year called a "jubilee" year. We encounter God's command in Leviticus 25:8-9:

"Count off seven Sabbath years – seven times seven years – so that the seven Sabbath years amount to a period of forty-nine years. Then have the trumpet sounded everywhere on the tenth day of the seventh month; on the Day of Atonement sound the trumpet throughout your land".

In terms of what we have studied throughout this book, we see the wonderful confluence of the idea of shemitah, of release from debts, and the reality of Atonement, that ability for all people to find at-one-ment with their Saviour God! The fiftieth, Jubilee year was a year of restoration, when not only financial debts were cancelled, but the 'reset button' was pressed once again! The Good News translation renders this quite well in its paraphrase style. Let us explore the full command:

"Count seven times seven years, a total of forty-nine years. Then, on the tenth day of the seventh month, the Day of Atonement, send someone to blow a trumpet throughout the whole land. In this way you shall set the fiftieth year apart and proclaim freedom to all the

inhabitants of the land. During this year all property that has been sold shall be restored to the original owner or the descendants, and any who have been sold as slaves shall return to their families.

You shall not plant your fields or harvest the grain that grows by itself or gather the grapes in your un-pruned vineyards. The whole year shall be sacred for you; you shall eat only what the fields produce of themselves. In this year all property that has been sold shall be restored to its original owner. So when you sell land to an Israelite or buy land, do not deal unfairly. The price is to be set according to the number of years the land can produce crops before the next Year of Restoration. If there are many years, the price shall be higher, but if there are only a few years, the price shall be lower, because what is being sold is the number of crops the land can produce. Do not cheat an Israelite, but obey the Lord your God. Obey all the Lord's laws and commands, so that you may live in safety in the land" (Leviticus 25:8-18, GNT).

In order to preserve the integrity of the tribes of Israel, and the family structure, there was to be a release and a restoration. Debts were released as in the 'ordinary' shemitah, but in the Jubilee year if a person had lost their inheritance then it would be restored to the family – if others had taken charge of land, then they had to relinquish it. Those sold as bond-servants were to be given their freedom. Possessions were to be returned to their rightful owners. Thus in Jubilee we see, once again, a "type" of the Messiah's completed work – to "restore" to God the Father those who had been enslaved by sin, to cancel *all* debts, to restore individuals to the position that God had always intended them to occupy.

The commencement of a Jubilee Year was proclaimed throughout the land on the Day of Atonement by means of trumpet (shofar) blasts – Leviticus 25:9. The activities that took place during a Jubilee Year were similar to those that were prescribed for the sabbatical year. To prevent abuse of the process through opportunism or financial speculation, the Israelites were specifically commanded to deal fairly and honestly with each other in the fear of God, Who was the real power in the land (Leviticus 25:14-17). As the old phrase has it, these things were done *with God as their witness* ....

Isaiah 61 reflects the idea of Jubilee. In some translations of the Bible the heading "The Year of the Lord's Favour" has been added by modern editors. In this chapter the year of the Lord's favour is spoken of (61:2) which is a year of vengeance for God, when wrongs will be righted and those who mourn will be provided a "crown of beauty instead of ashes" and "a garment of praise instead of a spirit of despair". As Bible readers we can be excused for asking ourselves, just who is it that refers to himself as "me" in Isaiah 61:1? Who is it that the Lord has anointed to preach good news to the poor, to bind up the broken hearted, and to proclaim freedom for captives and release for prisoners? Whilst we might possibly question his identity, Jesus had no such doubts. It is Him! Jesus quoted Isaiah 61 in Luke 4:18-19 and told His hearers that this scripture was today "fulfilled in your hearing". It is the Lord Yeshua (Jesus) that is the Father's instrument to inaugurate the *permanent* year of the Lord's favour, when those who are far away from God, those who have lost their inheritance of intimate relationship with their loving creator God, can have that relationship restored through Jesus the great Healer and Saviour. Jesus inaugurates and effects the everlasting *year of the Lord's favour*. Readers may wish to pause to read Isaiah chapter 61 and Luke 4:14-22.

Conclusion

It is probably fair to say that seven is a magnificent number in the Bible – indeed it truly is "the magnificent seven"! Far too often for mere coincidence, the number is associated with God providing a *complete* and *finished* message to us. In the Moedim we see the same truth; God's message of Jesus the Messiah is completely stated, completely illustrated, in those seven appointed times of the Lord. There is nothing more to be added.

Note

[1] We note with interest the popular books by Jonathan Cahn in the USA.

APPENDIX 5
OLD AND NEW

Historically, the community of believers in Jesus has labelled the Spirit-inspired Scriptures into two halves, with the perhaps confusing titles "Old Testament" and "New Testament". In some people's minds that has become "Old Testament" *versus* "New Testament". Some commentators say (correctly, it would seem) that this division of 'old' and 'new' is entirely artificial and slightly misleading – we have a single scripture and it is solely the testimony about the Messiah. If nothing else the use of the terms "old" and "new" suggests that the 'old' is somehow replaced by the 'new', in much the same way that an old shirt is replaced by a new one! This impression is incorrect in relation to the Scriptures. We observed in the introduction that "hand-in-glove" is perhaps the optimum way of understanding the pre-Incarnation and the post-Incarnation Scriptures.

Several alternative titles suggest themselves. Each has advantages and each has disadvantages.

Old Testament	New Testament	Comments
The Promise	The Promise Fulfilled	This reminds us that in the pre-Incarnation period, the primary purpose of the Tanakh is to point towards the coming Messiah – Who is THE promise. Once Jesus had fulfilled His mission, arguably the promise has been fulfilled. The disadvantage of this approach is that there are still, today, promises in the Old and New Testaments that remain yet to be fulfilled.
Tanakh	Brit Chadasha	This has the clarity that it is what Jewish people consider to be the two scriptures. It at least recognizes a distinct purpose for the two, seen from a Jewish viewpoint. We note of course the Jewish connection of all Scriptures. Brit Chadasha is Hebrew for "New Covenant".
Old Covenant	New Covenant	This is the terminology of the Orthodox stream of Christianity. Whilst in some ways it is technically correct, it contains the same disadvantages of "Old Testament" versus "New Testament". It tends to pitch them against each other. It also fails to answer clearly the question WHICH old covenant(s) are we talking about?
Old Witness	New Witness	The focus here is upon the witness of Scripture to eternal and unchangeable truth, where the witnessing is to God's outworked purposes PRIOR TO the time of Jesus, where the 'new witness' is precisely the eye witness accounts of Jesus and what might be called the proto-church period. The advantage is that it recognizes the idea of witness and the validity of witness testimony (as in a court of law). The disadvantage is that this is a little obscure in modern language.

Of course, in English the word "testament" has about it the idea of testimony – or of "witness". In a court of law a witness gives their testimony. Both Old and New Testaments "witness" to God's over-arching plan and purpose of salvation – of building a Kingdom (and a family) of all those who place their faith and trust in the Jewish Messiah.

God's purposes are both revealed and "legalised"[1] through the covenants, especially the Abraham, Moses, David and Messiah *progressive layers* of covenant. The term "new covenant" is expressed in Jeremiah 31:31. Some Christians are apt to use this term as a two-word justification for their idea that at some point *after* the Old Testament era, God would "ditch" His existing covenant(s) with Israel and replace them with a "new" covenant with the whole of mankind – not just the Jews.[2] This idea then has about it the belief that at some indeterminate point (probably at the crucifixion of Jesus) that the "new" covenant became effective, and simultaneously switched-off the old covenant(s). (The present author once received a stroppy email from an angry churchman who insisted there is only one Old Testament covenant and that it was "replaced" by one New Testament covenant. A convenient idea, if you have a "theology" to defend, but it fails at the most basic level: we have already seen in Appendix 3 that there are multiple layers to covenant revealed in the Old Testament. The One New Man Bible in its extensive glossary, lists no fewer than eighteen specific covenants in the Old Testament.)[3]

What then is the problem with this interpretation of Jeremiah 31:31? As always, we need to read Jeremiah 31:31 within its context. Verse 31 begins with the phrase "the days are coming" and goes on to express that, at some point in the future, God will write His laws directly onto men's hearts, so that, in a very real sense, these laws are internalised and become part of the make-up of the individual disciple of Jesus. So far, so good. We can all agree with that basic premise. However, it is clear that the "Christian Church" has sinned and rebelled against God in all the ways that the Hebrew people of the Old Testament rebelled. Can we then truly say that we today live in a New Covenant era that is completely different from the purported Old Covenant era? In what way are rebellious Christians "better" than their rebellious Jewish forebears? Something must be wrong with our common understanding of the wonderful Jeremiah 31:31 promise.

We come back to context: what is the over-arching context within which Jeremiah 31:31 is given? We need to ask, in the specific phrase "the days are coming" precisely what days are we speaking of. Here context helps us. We need to read and understand Jeremiah 31:31 in the context of Jeremiah chapters 30 through 31. Interestingly and usefully, the Roman Catholic New Jerusalem Bible brackets chapters 26 through 35 as a distinct group, which they head up as Part 3 of Jeremiah, PROPHESIES OF HAPPINESS. These chapters are then sub-divided into five sub-sections (A through E) and we find chapters 30 and 31 in the sub-section C headed up THE BOOK OF CONSOLATION. If we look then at chapters 30 and 31 we find something important.

In chapters 30 and 31 there are ten references to "those days", "that day", "in those days" and "the days are coming".[4] A careful and contextual reading of these chapters however makes it abundantly clear that these days lie in the future and the promises are as yet unfulfilled in their entirety. It is arguable that the context of these chapters refers in some way to the re-establishment of the modern state of Israel and the conclusion of the times of the Gentiles.[5] Whilst this may provide a partial fulfilment and partial understanding, yet the peace that is promised in these chapters is simply not here today – nor has it been here at any time during what some people like to think of as "the Christian era". So if it is clear that nine of the ten references lie at some time in the future (and indeed 30:24 helpfully makes the bald statement that we will not understand these things until "the final days" or "latter days" have arrived) then can we isolate Jeremiah 31:31 from the other references and claim – this prophecy is stand-alone and it is for today?!

The resolution to this problem (although it is a problem that few Christians are prepared to acknowledge) is straightforward: God's promise of peace is to be found in His Messiah Jesus. Through the infilling of the Holy Spirit we can claim with confidence that God's laws are indeed written in our hearts, and we are no longer dependent upon the externalities of the Law (or Torah). These externalities, some of which were time-limited in their application in any case,[6] are now indwelling the true disciple of Jesus. So today we do see a partial fulfilment of Jeremiah 31:31 and we can truly say that we live in the vanguard of the

New Covenant. It is coming and one day it will be here in permanence. Scholars point out helpfully that the correct translation of "new covenant" is actually "renewed covenant". This nuance is surely valid, though lack of space in this book means it is something we cannot explore in detail. This correct rendering does, however, allow the clear linkage between the renewed covenant and the earlier covenantal promises – none of which was abrogated by God. It is not that the "old" covenant (whatever that may mean in practice!) has been extinguished by a "new" one, but rather that all the old promises have been renewed to encompass all people who place their faith and trust in Jesus the Messiah. So we, as His disciples, are grafted into the benefits of the covenants and adopted to be a part of God's worldwide family.

We note finally that the New Testament (Brit Chadasha) is abundantly clear through the very precise writings of the (unknown) author of the Epistle to the Hebrews, in Hebrews chapter 8, that there is today a "better covenant" (8:6) of which we are the beneficiaries if we place our faith in Messiah Jesus. Hebrews chapter 8 indeed quotes Jeremiah 31:31 (Hebrews 8:8) and indicates that God is graciously saving the very best until last (verse 6). In verse 13 it states plainly and unequivocally:

By calling this covenant "new," he has made the first one obsolete; and what is obsolete and outdated will soon disappear. (NIV)

As this is an important verse and central to our argument, let us look at it in several standard translations:

In speaking of a new covenant, he makes the first one obsolete. And what is becoming obsolete and growing old is ready to vanish away. (ESV)

In speaking of a new covenant he treats the first as obsolete. And what is becoming obsolete and growing old is ready to vanish away. (RSV)

In that he saith, a new covenant, he hath made the first old. Now that which decayeth and waxeth old is ready to vanish away. (KJV)

When he says "New" he has made the first old: and the one that is old is near disappearing. (ONMB)

It is quite clear from each of these that the "old" is not yet gone. It is still in force and effect, but it is on its way out. We can call this "planned obsolescence", to use a decidedly modern term. God planned to supplant the covenants based on Law with one based on relationship. It is this relationship-based covenant that will guarantee eternal life and eternal righteousness, based on the completed work of Jesus accomplished at Golgotha – the place of the skull. It is through the blood of Jesus that we are spiritually "washed" clean forever (1 John 1:7).

Notes

[1] This is not Legalism! It means simply that because God has "cut" these covenants, they are 100% dependable – we do not have to 'fret' that they will be breached by God. God's promises are eternally dependable.

[2] This is the bedrock of the false idea today called "Replacement Theology"

[3] There is an excellent and extensive article on the covenants in the One New Man Bible. Recommended!

[4] Jeremiah 30:3; 30:8; 30:24; 31:1; 31:6; 31:27; 31:29; 31:31; 31:33; 31:38.

[5] Luke 21:24

[6] See for example Steve Maltz's useful book *God's Tapestry – What Do We Do With the Hebrew Scriptures?* (Saffron Planet Publishing, 2015).

SELECT BIBLIOGRAPHY

Bamber, Rosemary, *In Time With God* (In Time With God Publications, 2012), ISBN 978-09572871-1-2

Crombie, Kelvin, *In Covenant With Jesus* (Kelvin Crombie Mundaring, 2012), ISBN 978-09873630-0-8

Fuchs, Daniel, *Israel's Holy Days In Type and Prophecy* (Chosen People Ministries, 1985), ISBN 978-08721319-8-9

Jacob, Alex, *Receive The Truth* (Glory to Glory Publications, 2011), ISBN 978-09567831-0-3

Jacob, Alex, *The Case For Enlargement Theology*, second edition (Glory to Glory Publications, 2011), ISBN 978-09567831-1-0

Keller, Phillip, *A Shepherd Looks at The Lamb of God* (Bethany House, 1982), ISBN 0720805279

Pawson, David, *Unlocking the Bible* (HarperCollins Publishers, 2015 rpt), ISBN 978-000716666-4

Sadler, I A, *Mystery, Babylon The Great*, second edition (I A Sadler, 2006) [Note that this book was a private publication and does not bear an ISBN. However it is believed still to be available and a Google search may display sources.]

Stevenson, Greg 'The Message of The Shofar', CMJ Research Paper #8, November 2010 (available from CMJ UK)

NOT CITED IN THIS BOOK BUT OF INTEREST

A fascinating article entitled 'No One Knows The Day Or The Hour?' by Eddie Chumney. It explores and challenges the meaning behind Jesus' apparent statement that the timing of the return of the Messiah will be unknown (Matthew 24:36, Mark 13:32).

http://www.hebroots.org/hebrootsarchive/9807/980715_c.html